PLANT-BASED
MEDITERRANEAN

GARDEN of GRAPES.

First Edition: 2023

Published by Garden of Grapes.

Printed in USA

The recipes, techniques, and tips in this cookbook are intended for personal use only. The author and publisher are not responsible for any adverse effects or consequences resulting from the use of the recipes or suggestions in this book.

Library of Congress Cataloging-in-Publication Data:

First edition.
Includes index.

Manufactured in USA

Introduction

Ladies and gentlemen, epicureans, and all those with a passion for the flavors of the Mediterranean,

Welcome to the "Mediterranean Plant-Based Cookbook: From Olive Grove to Table." Here, nestled within these pages, you'll embark on a sensory journey that harks back to the sun-drenched landscapes, the azure waters, and the rich culinary traditions of the Mediterranean. It's a journey that elevates plant-based dining to an art form, celebrating the simplicity and robustness of this time-honored cuisine.

The Mediterranean holds a special place in my heart, a place where I've found solace, inspiration, and an endless array of sumptuous dishes that unite history, culture, and a love for fresh, vibrant ingredients. As the author of this cookbook, I'm thrilled to be your guide on this culinary adventure. I've spent countless hours in bustling markets, tiny family-owned restaurants, and bustling kitchens, absorbing the very essence of Mediterranean cooking.

The inspiration for this cookbook is twofold. First and foremost, it's a tribute to the bountiful and wholesome ingredients that grace the Mediterranean region. The fertile olive groves, vineyards, and fields teem with gifts from nature, and they serve as the foundation for a diet that's celebrated worldwide for its health benefits. But beyond that, it's a celebration of the Mediterranean lifestyle – the conviviality, the unhurried pace, and the sheer pleasure of savoring a good meal with friends and family.

Within these pages, you'll find a treasure trove of plant-based Mediterranean dishes that reflect the diverse cultures and flavors of the region. From the exquisite simplicity of Greek salads bursting with flavor to the hearty stews of North Africa and the aromatic spices of the Middle East, every recipe has been meticulously crafted to capture the essence of the Mediterranean.

As you delve into this cookbook, you can expect to find a vast array of recipes that cater to every occasion. Whether you're hosting a festive gathering, planning a romantic dinner, or simply seeking inspiration for your everyday meals, these pages hold the key to vibrant, wholesome, and utterly satisfying plant-based dishes. Alongside each recipe, you'll find vivid pictures that offer a glimpse into the tantalizing world of Mediterranean cuisine.

So, my fellow culinary explorers, I invite you to embrace the Mediterranean way of life through the art of plant-based cooking. As you embark on this adventure, you'll discover that the Mediterranean isn't just a place on a map; it's a way of life, a philosophy of dining, and a celebration of the natural world. Through each recipe, you'll feel the sun on your face, hear the waves lapping the shore, and savor the rich flavors that the Mediterranean so generously offers.

Prepare to be inspired, to delight your senses, and to savor every bite. The journey begins now. Welcome to the Mediterranean. Bon appétit!

Cooking Philosophy or Approach

My friends,

Allow me to share with you a glimpse into the heart and soul of the "Mediterranean Plant-Based Cookbook: From Olive Grove to Table." As you've ventured into this world of flavors, where the azure waters of the Mediterranean meet the fertile soils of ancient lands, I want to reveal the culinary philosophy that guides our journey.

Our approach to cooking and food is an embodiment of simplicity and authenticity. We draw inspiration from the time-honored traditions of Mediterranean cuisine, respecting the heritage that has been passed down through generations. This cookbook is more than just a collection of recipes; it's an ode to a way of life.

In the Mediterranean, we believe in letting the ingredients shine. Fresh, seasonal produce picked at the peak of ripeness is our canvas. We use vibrant and flavorful herbs, the golden nectar of pure olive oil, and the whisper of sea salt to accentuate the natural essence of each ingredient. It's about letting the ingredients speak for themselves, for they have stories to tell.

It's not just about eating; it's about savoring. Every meal is an opportunity to indulge in the simple pleasures of life. We savor each bite, enjoying the textures and flavors that the Mediterranean bounty offers. We share our meals with loved ones, for we believe that food has the power to connect hearts and create lasting memories.

We also respect the environment and our own well-being. Our recipes embrace the plant-based way of life, honoring the balance of nature and the nourishment it provides. We celebrate the flavors of fresh vegetables, legumes, grains, and fruits. With each dish, we aim to showcase the abundant plant-based delights that the Mediterranean region has to offer.

As for techniques, our style is both time-honored and contemporary. We pay homage to ancient methods like slow roasting and simmering, allowing the ingredients to meld together harmoniously. At the same time, we embrace modern tools and methods, making these culinary traditions accessible to you in your kitchen. Each recipe is a delightful fusion of tradition and innovation, just like the Mediterranean itself.

And so, as you embark on this voyage through our cookbook, remember that each recipe is not just a meal; it's a story. A story of culture, tradition, and a love for the simple, exquisite beauty of Mediterranean flavors. You're not just cooking; you're creating an experience, embracing the Mediterranean spirit, and indulging in the very essence of life itself.

May your culinary adventures be filled with joy and the delectable flavors of the Mediterranean. As you dive into these recipes, may you not only nourish your body but also your soul. That, my friends, is the heart and soul of our cookbook.

Vegan Mediterranean Breakfast Sandwich
See page, 5

Tips for Successful Cooking

Hey there, fellow culinary travelers,

As you embark on this journey through the pages of the "Mediterranean Plant-Based Cookbook: From Olive Grove to Table," you're stepping into a world of flavors, aromas, and traditions that have withstood the test of time. The Mediterranean, with its rich history and diverse cultures, has blessed the world with some of the most delectable dishes. It's a land where the olive groves whisper tales of centuries gone by, and where the table is a sacred place for family and friends to come together.

To ensure your adventure in the kitchen is as smooth as the sea at sunrise, I've put together a few tips and tricks that'll serve you well in your culinary endeavors. These are the little secrets that transform ordinary cooking into an extraordinary experience.

1. The Fresher, the Better:
When it comes to Mediterranean cuisine, freshness is key. Whether it's the ripest tomatoes, just-picked herbs, or the highest-quality olive oil you can lay your hands on, choose the freshest ingredients. It's like having the best canvas for your culinary masterpiece.

2. The Art of Seasoning:
The Mediterranean is a region where seasoning isn't just a step in the process; it's an art form. Herbs like basil, oregano, and thyme, along with spices like cumin and coriander, play pivotal roles. Don't be shy; season your dishes with confidence.

3. A Marriage of Flavors:
Mediterranean cooking excels at the harmonious marriage of ingredients. Think of a Caprese salad - tomatoes, mozzarella, basil, olive oil, and balsamic vinegar. Each ingredient shines while complementing the others. Embrace this approach, and you'll create dishes that sing with flavor.

4. Olive Oil: Liquid Gold:
The olive tree is an icon of the Mediterranean, and its oil is its liquid gold. Invest in a good-quality extra-virgin olive oil; it's a staple in Mediterranean cooking. Use it in dressings, drizzle it over finished dishes, and let it elevate your meals.

5. Don't Rush the Slow:

The Mediterranean way of cooking often involves slow simmering, braising, or roasting. It allows flavors to meld and intensify. So, don't rush through recipes. Take your time and savor the process.

6. Grains and Legumes:

The Mediterranean diet is rich in grains like couscous, bulgur, and quinoa, as well as legumes like chickpeas and lentils. These are not only nutritious but also incredibly versatile.

7. The Magic of Mezze:

Consider serving your dishes mezze-style, with a variety of small plates. It's a communal way to dine, encouraging sharing and conversation.

8. Wine and Dine:

Wine pairs beautifully with Mediterranean cuisine. Whether it's a crisp white wine or a robust red, a glass of vino can elevate your meal.

9. Don't Fear Experimentation:

While tradition is important, don't hesitate to add your own twist. The Mediterranean welcomes creativity in the kitchen.

10. The Spirit of Sharing:

Finally, remember that Mediterranean cuisine is about sharing. It's about bringing people together. So, invite your loved ones to the table, pour some wine, and create memories through the magic of food.

Now that you've armed yourself with these pearls of wisdom, I have every confidence that your journey through the Mediterranean's culinary wonders will be nothing short of extraordinary. May your kitchen be filled with the sounds of laughter, the clinking of glasses, and the wonderful aroma of dishes inspired by this remarkable region.

Buon appetito, or as they say in the Mediterranean, Kali orexi (bon appétit)!

Vegan Italian Pasta Bowl
See page, 38

Kitchen Essentials

Ladies and gentlemen, home chefs and aspiring culinary artists,

Before you embark on your odyssey through the vibrant and flavorful recipes contained within the "Mediterranean Plant-Based Cookbook: From Olive Grove to Table," let's ensure your kitchen is well-prepared for this exciting journey. Mediterranean cuisine beckons with its sun-kissed flavors and a fusion of wholesome ingredients. To truly immerse yourself in this experience, you'll want to equip your kitchen with some essential tools and master their use.

Essential Kitchen Tools and Equipment:

1. Chef's Knife: The cornerstone of your culinary arsenal, a sharp and reliable chef's knife will be your trusted companion for chopping, dicing, and slicing the fresh produce so essential in Mediterranean cooking.

2. Cutting Board: Invest in a durable and spacious cutting board to provide a stable surface for your knife work. We recommend using separate boards for vegetables and proteins to maintain the integrity of your ingredients.

3. Food Processor: This versatile appliance will help you create smooth hummus, zesty pesto, and finely chopped herbs with ease. A must for Mediterranean dips and spreads.

4. Citrus Juicer: Whether it's lemons, oranges, or even pomegranates, a citrus juicer ensures you can extract every drop of that liquid gold, adding a burst of Mediterranean freshness to your dishes.

5. Garlic Press: Mediterranean cuisine loves garlic! A garlic press simplifies the task of crushing garlic cloves, infusing your dishes with that irresistible aroma and flavor.

6. Zester/Grater: To enhance your recipes with the bright and zesty appeal of citrus fruits and Mediterranean cheeses, a quality zester or grater is indispensable.

7. Mortar and Pestle: Ideal for grinding whole spices and herbs into aromatic blends. You'll need this for creating classic Mediterranean seasoning mixes.

8. Baking Sheets: Mediterranean dishes often require roasting, so invest in sturdy baking sheets for evenly cooked vegetables and delectable baked goods.

Tips on Using Your Kitchen Tools Effectively:

- Knife Skills: Sharpen your knife skills, ensuring you can confidently slice, dice, and chop. A good grip and proper technique will save time and ensure safety in the kitchen.

- Blade Maintenance: Keep your chef's knife sharp with regular honing and sharpening. A dull knife is not only less efficient but can also be dangerous.

- Citrus Juicing: To get the most juice from citrus fruits, roll them on the countertop while applying slight pressure before cutting and juicing.

- Garlic Preparation: To peel garlic more easily, place a clove under the flat side of your chef's knife and press down gently. The skin will loosen, allowing for effortless peeling.

- Zesting: When zesting citrus fruits, be cautious not to grate the bitter white pith, as it can detract from the vibrant flavors you're aiming to capture.

- Mortar and Pestle Techniques: For effective use of the mortar and pestle, use a gentle but consistent grinding motion. Small, circular movements yield the best results for creating Mediterranean spice blends.

With these essential tools at your disposal and the knowledge of how to use them effectively, you're primed for a Mediterranean culinary adventure. Prepare your senses for the captivating flavors and aromas of this rich and diverse cuisine. Happy cooking, and bon appétit!

Vegan Spanish Rice Bowl
See page, 42

Flavor Pairing Suggestions

Alright, my friends and fellow culinary enthusiasts,

As we bid adieu to this journey through the Mediterranean flavorscape, I want to ensure that your culinary voyage doesn't conclude with the last page of this cookbook. Cooking, you see, is a form of art, a canvas where you can blend and pair flavors, colors, and textures to create your masterpieces.

So, let's talk about flavor pairing, the secret alchemy of every great cook. Think of it as a melodic composition, where ingredients are the instruments, and you, my fellow chef, are the conductor. In the Mediterranean, we celebrate fresh, vibrant, and robust flavors that harmonize beautifully, like a symphony of culinary wonders.

1. Tomatoes and Basil: Ah, the classic duo! Tomatoes' juicy acidity and basil's fresh, herbal notes are a match made in culinary heaven. Slice those tomatoes and layer them with basil leaves. Drizzle some olive oil and sprinkle sea salt. Now, that's a caprese salad to remember.

2. Lemon and Garlic: The zesty brightness of lemon and the earthy pungency of garlic play together like a comedy duo. A squeeze of lemon and a clove of minced garlic can transform any dish, from roasted veggies to a simple pasta.

3. Mint and Cucumber: Cool as a Mediterranean breeze, this pairing is perfect for refreshing salads and tzatziki. Muddle some mint leaves, slice cucumbers, and let them mingle. Add some yogurt or vinegar for a tangy twist.

4. Chickpeas and Tahini: Creamy, nutty, and oh-so-versatile. Chickpeas and tahini combine to create the silky wonder that is hummus. They're also a delightful base for Mediterranean bowls, wraps, and salads.

5. Rosemary and Roasted Potatoes: When rosemary meets roasted potatoes, something magical happens. The earthiness of rosemary infuses into the starchy potatoes, creating a side dish that's a favorite in every Mediterranean home.

6. Cumin and Coriander: These spices add depth to Mediterranean stews and dishes. A pinch of cumin and a dash of coriander can transport your taste buds to North Africa.

7. Olive Oil and Everything: The golden elixir of Mediterranean cuisine, olive oil, goes with just about anything. Drizzle it over a salad, use it to sauté, or dip your bread in it. Its fruity, robust flavor elevates any dish.

Now, my friends, take these flavor pairings and experiment. Craft your culinary masterpieces and relish the journey. The Mediterranean kitchen is a treasure trove of tastes, and you hold the key. Combine, create, and savor the magic of Mediterranean flavors in your own unique way.

Remember, the best recipes are often the ones you create yourself. So, venture into your kitchen with a curious heart and a daring spirit. Who knows what Mediterranean wonders you'll discover on your plate?

Wishing you countless delicious moments in your culinary adventures,

INDEX

Chapter 1
Mediterranean Breakfasts

2 bowls   350   15 min

Vegan Mediterranean Breakfast Bowl

Easy

A vibrant bowl of flavors inspired by the Mediterranean coast. Enjoy a hearty mix of fresh veggies, olives, and hummus.

Ingredients:

- 1 cup cooked quinoa
- 1 cup chickpeas, drained
- 1/2 cup cherry tomatoes, halved
- 1/4 cup cucumber, diced
- 2 tbsp Kalamata olives, sliced
- 2 tbsp hummus
- 1 tbsp olive oil
- 1 tsp lemon juice
- Salt and pepper to taste

Directions

1. Cook quinoa according to package instructions.
2. In a bowl, combine quinoa, chickpeas, tomatoes, cucumber, and olives.
3. Drizzle with olive oil and lemon juice. Season with salt and pepper.
4. Top with hummus.
5. Serve and enjoy!

Substitutions

- Chickpea allergies

2
servings

280

30 min

Vegan Shakshuka

Ingredients:

- 1 tbsp olive oil
- 1 onion, chopped
- 1 red bell pepper, diced
- 2 cloves garlic, minced
- 1 can (14 oz) crushed tomatoes
- 2 tsp cumin
- 1 tsp paprika
- 1/2 tsp chili powder
- Salt and pepper to taste
- 4 eggs
- Fresh parsley, for garnish

Normal

A spicy and savory North African dish. Perfect for brunch!

Directions

1. Heat olive oil in a skillet. Add onions and bell pepper, sauté until soft.
2. Stir in garlic, cumin, paprika, and chili powder.
3. Pour in crushed tomatoes. Simmer for 10 min.
4. Make small wells in the sauce and crack eggs into them.
5. Cover and cook until eggs are set.
6. Garnish with parsley.
7. Serve hot.

Substitutions

- Vegan cheese for eggs

2
servings

240

20 min

Vegan Greek Tofu Scramble

Easy

A plant-based twist on a Greek classic.

Ingredients:

- 1/2 block firm tofu, crumbled
- 1/2 red onion, chopped
- 1/2 red bell pepper, diced
- 1/2 cup spinach
- 1/4 cup Kalamata olives, sliced
- 1/4 cup cherry tomatoes, halved
- 2 tbsp nutritional yeast
- 1 tsp dried oregano
- Salt and pepper to taste
- Olive oil for cooking

Directions

1. Heat olive oil in a pan. Sauté onions and bell peppers until soft.
2. Add crumbled tofu, olives, and tomatoes. Cook for 5 min.
3. Stir in nutritional yeast, oregano, salt, and pepper.
4. Add spinach and cook until wilted.
5. Serve hot.

Substitutions

- Spinach for kale

2 sandwic hes **420** **15 min**

Vegan Mediterranean Breakfast Sandwich

Ingredients:

- 4 slices whole-grain bread
- 1/2 cup hummus
- 1/2 cucumber, thinly sliced
- 1/2 cup baby spinach
- 1/4 cup sun-dried tomatoes, sliced
- 1/4 cup roasted red pepper, sliced
- Salt and pepper to taste

Super Easy

A handheld delight with the flavors of the Mediterranean.

Directions

1. Toast the bread slices.
2. Spread hummus on each slice.
3. Layer cucumber, spinach, sun-dried tomatoes, and roasted red pepper.
4. Season with salt and pepper.
5. Assemble into sandwiches.
6. Serve and enjoy!

Substitutions

- Use pita bread

4
servings

320

40 min

Vegan Spanish Potato Omelette

Ingredients:

- 2 cups potatoes, thinly sliced
- 1 cup chickpea flour
- 1/2 cup water
- 1/2 onion, thinly sliced
- 2 cloves garlic, minced
- 2 tbsp olive oil
- 1 tsp turmeric
- Salt and pepper to taste

Normal

A vegan twist on the classic Spanish omelette.

Directions

1. Heat olive oil in a skillet. Add potatoes, onions, and garlic. Cook until tender.
2. In a bowl, mix chickpea flour, water, turmeric, salt, and pepper.
3. Pour the batter over the cooked potatoes.
4. Cook until set, flipping once.
5. Slice and serve hot.

Substitutions

- Use sweet potatoes instead

2
servings

290

20 min

Vegan Mediterranean Quinoa Breakfast

Ingredients:

- 1 cup cooked quinoa
- 1/2 cup cucumber, diced
- 1/2 cup cherry tomatoes, halved
- 1/4 cup red onion, finely chopped
- 1/4 cup Kalamata olives, sliced
- 1/4 cup fresh parsley, chopped
- 2 tbsp lemon juice
- 1 tbsp olive oil
- Salt and pepper to taste

Substitutions

- Add diced bell peppers

A protein-packed breakfast bowl with Mediterranean flair.

Directions

1. In a bowl, combine quinoa, cucumber, tomatoes, onion, olives, and parsley.
2. In a separate bowl, whisk together lemon juice and olive oil.
3. Drizzle the dressing over the quinoa mixture.
4. Season with salt and pepper.
5. Serve and enjoy!

2 servings

220

15 min

Easy

Vegan Moroccan Spiced Oatmeal

Ingredients:

- 1 cup rolled oats
- 2 cups almond milk
- 1/4 cup dried apricots, chopped
- 2 tbsp maple syrup
- 1 tsp cinnamon
- 1/2 tsp ground ginger
- 1/4 tsp ground cardamom
- Pinch of salt
- Chopped nuts for garnish (optional)

Warm and comforting oatmeal infused with Moroccan spices.

Directions

1. In a saucepan, combine oats, almond milk, apricots, maple syrup, and spices.
2. Cook over medium heat until thickened.
3. Add a pinch of salt.
4. Serve hot, garnished with chopped nuts if desired.

Substitutions

- Use raisins instead of apricots

2 servings **380** **25 min**

Vegan Turkish Breakfast Platter

Ingredients:

- 1/2 cup hummus
- 1/2 cup baba ganoush
- 1/4 cup tabbouleh salad
- 1/4 cup cucumber, sliced
- 1/4 cup cherry tomatoes, halved
- 2-4 olives, for garnish
- Fresh pita bread
- Fresh mint leaves, for garnish

Easy

A delightful spread of Turkish flavors for a hearty breakfast.

Directions

1. Arrange hummus, baba ganoush, tabbouleh, cucumber, and tomatoes on a platter.
2. Garnish with olives and mint leaves.
3. Serve with warm pita bread.
4. Enjoy the Mediterranean feast!

Substitutions

- Use store-bought hummus

4
servings

280

35 min

Normal

Vegan Italian Frittata

Ingredients:

- 2 cups chickpea flour
- 2 cups water
- 1/2 cup cherry tomatoes, halved
- 1/4 cup spinach, chopped
- 1/4 cup red bell pepper, diced
- 1/4 cup red onion, finely chopped
- 1/4 cup nutritional yeast
- 2 cloves garlic, minced
- 2 tsp dried basil
- Salt and pepper to taste
- Olive oil for cooking

A savory frittata with Italian flavors and no eggs.

Directions

1. Preheat oven to 375°F (190°C).
2. In a blender, combine chickpea flour, water, nutritional yeast, garlic, basil, salt, and pepper. Blend until smooth.
3. In an oven-safe skillet, heat olive oil. Add tomatoes, spinach, bell pepper, and onion. Sauté for a few minutes.
4. Pour chickpea flour mixture over the veggies.
5. Bake for 25-30 minutes until set.
6. Slice and serve.

Substitutions
- Add mushrooms for extra flavor

2 wraps   320   20 min

Easy

Vegan Lebanese Breakfast Wrap

A portable breakfast wrap inspired by Lebanese flavors.

Ingredients:

- 2 large whole-grain tortillas
- 1 cup cooked quinoa
- 1/2 cup hummus
- 1/4 cup cucumber, sliced
- 1/4 cup cherry tomatoes, halved
- 1/4 cup fresh parsley, chopped
- 2 tbsp tahini
- 2 tbsp lemon juice
- Salt and pepper to taste

Directions

1. Warm tortillas in a pan.
2. Spread hummus on each tortilla.
3. Layer with quinoa, cucumber, tomatoes, and parsley.
4. Drizzle with tahini and lemon juice.
5. Season with salt and pepper.
6. Wrap and enjoy!

Substitutions

- Use lavash bread

Chapter 2
Mediterranean Lunches

4 servings

250

20 min

Easy

Vegan Greek Salad with Tofu Feta

A refreshing Greek salad with a twist – tofu feta adds creaminess.

Ingredients:

- 1 block extra-firm tofu, crumbled
- 2 cups cucumber, diced
- 2 cups cherry tomatoes, halved
- 1/2 red onion, thinly sliced
- 1/4 cup Kalamata olives, sliced
- 1/4 cup fresh parsley, chopped
- 3 tbsp olive oil
- 2 tbsp red wine vinegar
- 1 tsp dried oregano
- Salt and pepper to taste

Directions

1. In a bowl, mix tofu, cucumber, tomatoes, onion, olives, and parsley.
2. In a separate bowl, whisk together olive oil, red wine vinegar, oregano, salt, and pepper.
3. Drizzle dressing over the salad.
4. Toss gently and serve.

Substitutions

- Use store-bought vegan feta

2 wraps   380   30 min

Vegan Falafel Wrap with Tahini Sauce

Normal

A classic Mediterranean wrap featuring crispy falafel and creamy tahini sauce.

Ingredients:

- 4 falafel patties
- 2 large whole-grain tortillas
- 1/2 cup hummus
- 1/2 cup cucumber, thinly sliced
- 1/2 cup cherry tomatoes, halved
- 1/4 cup red onion, thinly sliced
- 2 tbsp tahini
- 2 tbsp lemon juice
- Salt and pepper to taste

Directions

1. Heat falafel patties according to package instructions.
2. Warm tortillas in a pan.
3. Spread hummus on each tortilla.
4. Layer with falafel, cucumber, tomatoes, and onion.
5. Drizzle with tahini and lemon juice.
6. Season with salt and pepper.
7. Wrap and enjoy!

Substitutions

- Make homemade falafel

2 wraps   320   15 min

Vegan Hummus and Veggie Wrap

Ingredients:

- 2 large whole-grain tortillas
- 1 cup hummus
- 1 cup cucumber, thinly sliced
- 1 cup red bell pepper, thinly sliced
- 1 cup baby spinach
- 1/4 cup red onion, thinly sliced
- 2 tbsp lemon juice
- Salt and pepper to taste

Substitutions

- Use flavored hummus

A simple yet satisfying wrap filled with creamy hummus and fresh veggies.

Directions

1. Warm tortillas in a pan.
2. Spread hummus on each tortilla.
3. Layer with cucumber, bell pepper, spinach, and onion.
4. Drizzle with lemon juice.
5. Season with salt and pepper.
6. Wrap and enjoy!

4
servings

220

40 min

Vegan Lentil Soup with Lemon

Normal

A comforting lentil soup with a Mediterranean twist, brightened by lemon.

Ingredients:

- 1 cup dried green lentils, rinsed
- 1 onion, chopped
- 2 carrots, chopped
- 2 cloves garlic, minced
- 4 cups vegetable broth
- 2 cups water
- 2 tsp cumin
- 1 tsp coriander
- 1/2 tsp turmeric
- Juice of 1 lemon
- Salt and pepper to taste

Directions

1. In a large pot, sauté onion and garlic until translucent.
2. Add lentils, carrots, vegetable broth, water, and spices.
3. Simmer for 30 min until lentils are tender.
4. Stir in lemon juice, salt, and pepper.
5. Serve hot.

Substitutions

- Add spinach for greens

4 servings   **280** kcal   **25 min**

Easy

Vegan Mediterranean Couscous Salad

Ingredients:

- 1 cup couscous
- 1 1/2 cups vegetable broth
- 1 cup cucumber, diced
- 1 cup cherry tomatoes, halved
- 1/2 cup Kalamata olives, sliced
- 1/4 cup red onion, finely chopped
- 1/4 cup fresh parsley, chopped
- 3 tbsp olive oil
- 2 tbsp lemon juice
- Salt and pepper to taste

A light and zesty couscous salad bursting with Mediterranean flavors.

Directions

1. In a saucepan, bring vegetable broth to a boil.
2. Stir in couscous, cover, and remove from heat. Let it sit for 5 min.
3. Fluff couscous with a fork and let it cool.
4. In a bowl, combine couscous, cucumber, tomatoes, olives, onion, and parsley.
5. In a separate bowl, whisk together olive oil, lemon juice, salt, and pepper.
6. Drizzle dressing over the salad.
7. Toss gently and serve.

Substitutions

- Use quinoa for couscous

4
servings

320

20 min

Vegan Italian Panzanella Salad

Ingredients:

- 4 cups stale whole-grain bread, cubed
- 2 cups cherry tomatoes, halved
- 1 cup cucumber, diced
- 1/4 cup red onion, thinly sliced
- 1/4 cup fresh basil, torn
- 3 tbsp olive oil
- 2 tbsp red wine vinegar
- 1 clove garlic, minced
- Salt and pepper to taste

Easy

A Tuscan bread salad with a vegan twist, featuring fresh tomatoes and basil.

Directions

1. In a large bowl, combine bread, tomatoes, cucumber, onion, and basil.
2. In a small bowl, whisk together olive oil, red wine vinegar, garlic, salt, and pepper.
3. Drizzle dressing over the salad.
4. Toss gently and let it sit for 10 min to allow the flavors to meld.
5. Serve and enjoy!

Substitutions

- Use ciabatta bread

4
servings

220

15 min

Vegan Tabouleh Salad

Easy

A classic Middle Eastern salad featuring fresh herbs and bulgur wheat.

Ingredients:

- 1 cup bulgur wheat
- 2 cups boiling water
- 1 cup fresh parsley, chopped
- 1/2 cup fresh mint leaves, chopped
- 2 cups tomatoes, diced
- 1/2 cup cucumber, diced
- 1/4 cup red onion, finely chopped
- 3 tbsp olive oil
- 2 tbsp lemon juice
- Salt and pepper to taste

Directions

1. Place bulgur wheat in a bowl and pour boiling water over it. Cover and let it sit for 10 min.
2. Fluff bulgur with a fork and let it cool.
3. In a large bowl, combine bulgur, parsley, mint, tomatoes, cucumber, and onion.
4. In a separate bowl, whisk together olive oil, lemon juice, salt, and pepper.
5. Drizzle dressing over the salad.
6. Toss gently and serve.

Substitutions

- Use quinoa for bulgur

4
servings

280

40 min

Vegan Greek Stuffed Peppers

Ingredients:

- 4 bell peppers, any color
- 1 cup cooked rice
- 1 cup chickpeas, drained
- 1/2 cup cherry tomatoes, halved
- 1/4 cup Kalamata olives, sliced
- 1/4 cup red onion, finely chopped
- 2 cloves garlic, minced
- 2 tbsp fresh parsley, chopped
- 2 tbsp olive oil
- 1 tsp dried oregano
- Salt and pepper to taste

Substitutions

- Use quinoa instead of rice

Bell peppers stuffed with a flavorful mixture of rice, veggies, and herbs.

Directions

1. Preheat oven to 375°F (190°C).
2. Cut the tops off the peppers and remove seeds.
3. In a bowl, mix cooked rice, chickpeas, tomatoes, olives, onion, garlic, parsley, olive oil, oregano, salt, and pepper.
4. Stuff the peppers with the mixture.
5. Place stuffed peppers in a baking dish, cover with foil, and bake for 25-30 min until peppers are tender.
6. Serve hot.

4 servings | 320 kcal | 45 min

Vegan Spanakopita Triangles

Ingredients:

- 8 sheets phyllo dough
- 2 cups spinach, chopped
- 1/2 block firm tofu, crumbled
- 1/4 cup nutritional yeast
- 1/4 cup red onion, finely chopped
- 2 cloves garlic, minced
- 2 tbsp fresh dill, chopped
- 2 tbsp olive oil
- Salt and pepper to taste

Substitutions

- Use store-bought phyllo dough

Normal

Crispy pastry triangles filled with a savory spinach and tofu mixture.

Directions

1. Preheat oven to 350°F (175°C).
2. In a skillet, sauté spinach, tofu, nutritional yeast, onion, garlic, and dill until spinach wilts.
3. Lay one sheet of phyllo dough flat and brush with olive oil. Add another sheet on top and repeat.
4. Cut the layered sheets into squares.
5. Place a spoonful of the spinach-tofu mixture in the center of each square.
6. Fold into triangles and place on a baking sheet.
7. Bake for 15-20 min until golden brown.
8. Serve warm.

4
servings

260

35 min

Vegan Eggplant Caponata

Ingredients:

- 2 eggplants, diced
- 1 can (14 oz) crushed tomatoes
- 1/2 cup Kalamata olives, sliced
- 1/4 cup capers
- 1/4 cup red onion, finely chopped
- 2 cloves garlic, minced
- 2 tbsp olive oil
- 2 tbsp red wine vinegar
- 2 tbsp fresh basil, chopped
- Salt and pepper to taste

A savory and sweet Sicilian dish with eggplant, tomatoes, and olives.

Directions

1. Heat olive oil in a large skillet.
2. Add eggplant and sauté until browned.
3. Stir in crushed tomatoes, olives, capers, onion, garlic, and vinegar.
4. Simmer for 15 min until the sauce thickens.
5. Season with salt, pepper, and fresh basil.
6. Serve hot or at room temperature.

Substitutions

- Use green olives

Chapter 3
Mediterranean Dinners

4 servings

320

45 min

Vegan Mediterranean Stuffed Bell Peppers

Ingredients:

- 4 bell peppers, any color
- 1 cup cooked rice
- 1 cup chickpeas, drained
- 1/2 cup cherry tomatoes, halved
- 1/4 cup Kalamata olives, sliced
- 1/4 cup red onion, finely chopped
- 2 cloves garlic, minced
- 2 tbsp fresh parsley, chopped
- 2 tbsp olive oil
- 1 tsp dried oregano
- Salt and pepper to taste

Substitutions

- Use quinoa instead of rice

Normal

Bell peppers filled with a Mediterranean-inspired mixture of rice, vegetables, and herbs.

Directions

1. Preheat oven to 375°F (190°C).
2. Cut the tops off the peppers and remove seeds.
3. In a bowl, mix cooked rice, chickpeas, tomatoes, olives, onion, garlic, parsley, olive oil, oregano, salt, and pepper.
4. Stuff the peppers with the mixture.
5. Place stuffed peppers in a baking dish, cover with foil, and bake for 25-30 min until peppers are tender.
6. Serve hot.

6
servings

380

60 min

Vegan Greek Moussaka

Ingredients:

- 2 eggplants, sliced
- 2 potatoes, sliced
- 1 cup green lentils, cooked
- 1 can (14 oz) crushed tomatoes
- 1/4 cup red onion, finely chopped
- 2 cloves garlic, minced
- 2 tbsp olive oil
- 2 tsp dried oregano
- 1 tsp cinnamon
- Salt and pepper to taste
- For the béchamel sauce:
- 2 cups almond milk
- 1/4 cup all-purpose flour
- 2 tbsp nutritional yeast
- 1/4 tsp nutmeg

Substitutions

- Use zucchini instead of eggplant

Normal

A classic Greek dish with layers of eggplant, potatoes, lentils, and a creamy béchamel sauce.

Directions

1. Preheat oven to 375°F (190°C).
2. Toss eggplant and potatoes with olive oil, salt, and pepper. Roast for 20 min.
3. In a skillet, sauté onion and garlic until soft.
4. Add lentils, crushed tomatoes, oregano, cinnamon, salt, and pepper. Simmer for 15 min.
5. In a saucepan, whisk together almond milk, flour, nutritional yeast, and nutmeg until thickened.
6. In a baking dish, layer roasted vegetables, lentil mixture, and béchamel sauce.
7. Repeat the layers.
8. Bake for 30 min until golden brown.
9. Serve hot.

6
servings

340

50 min

Vegan Italian Vegetable Lasagna

Normal

Layers of lasagna noodles, sautéed vegetables, marinara sauce, and vegan cheese, baked to perfection.

Ingredients:

- 9 lasagna noodles, cooked
- 2 cups marinara sauce
- 1 cup zucchini, sliced
- 1 cup bell peppers, thinly sliced
- 1 cup mushrooms, sliced
- 1/2 cup red onion, thinly sliced
- 2 cloves garlic, minced
- 1 1/2 cups vegan mozzarella cheese
- 1/4 cup fresh basil, chopped
- Olive oil for cooking
- Salt and pepper to taste

Directions

1. Preheat oven to 375°F (190°C).
2. In a skillet, sauté zucchini, bell peppers, mushrooms, onion, and garlic until tender.
3. In a baking dish, layer marinara sauce, cooked lasagna noodles, sautéed vegetables, vegan mozzarella cheese, and fresh basil.
4. Repeat the layers.
5. Bake for 25-30 min until cheese is bubbly and golden brown.
6. Serve hot.

Substitutions

- Use gluten-free lasagna noodles

4
servings

300

50 min

Normal

Vegan Moroccan Tagine with Chickpeas

Ingredients:

- 1 cup couscous
- 1 1/2 cups vegetable broth
- 1 can (14 oz) chickpeas, drained
- 1 cup butternut squash, diced
- 1 cup zucchini, diced
- 1/2 cup red bell pepper, diced
- 1/2 cup onion, finely chopped
- 2 cloves garlic, minced
- 2 tbsp olive oil
- 2 tsp ground cumin
- 1 tsp ground coriander
- 1/2 tsp ground cinnamon
- 1/4 tsp cayenne pepper
- Salt and pepper to taste

Substitutions

- Use sweet potatoes instead of squash

A fragrant Moroccan tagine featuring chickpeas, vegetables, and a blend of spices, served over couscous.

Directions

1. In a saucepan, bring vegetable broth to a boil.
2. Stir in couscous, cover, and remove from heat. Let it sit for 5 min.
3. Fluff couscous with a fork and let it cool.
4. In a tagine or large skillet, sauté onion and garlic in olive oil until soft.
5. Add chickpeas, butternut squash, zucchini, and bell pepper. Cook for 5 min.
6. Stir in ground cumin, ground coriander, ground cinnamon, cayenne pepper, salt, and pepper.
7. Simmer for 10 min until vegetables are tender.
8. Serve tagine over couscous.

4 servings

360

40 min

Vegan Lebanese Falafel Plate

A Lebanese feast with crispy falafel, creamy tahini sauce, tabbouleh salad, and warm pita bread.

Ingredients:

- 16 falafel patties (store-bought or homemade)
- 4 whole-grain pita bread
- 1 cup tabbouleh salad (store-bought or homemade)
- 1/2 cup hummus (store-bought or homemade)
- 1/4 cup tahini sauce (store-bought or homemade)
- 1/4 cup cucumber, sliced
- 1/4 cup cherry tomatoes, halved
- Fresh parsley for garnish
- Olive oil for frying (if making homemade falafel)

Directions

1. If making homemade falafel, heat olive oil in a pan. Fry falafel patties until golden brown.
2. Warm pita bread in a pan.
3. Serve falafel with pita bread, tabbouleh salad, hummus, tahini sauce, cucumber, and cherry tomatoes.
4. Garnish with fresh parsley.
5. Enjoy the Lebanese flavors!

Substitutions

- Use store-bought falafel

4
servings

280

35 min

Vegan Mediterranean Chickpea Stew

Normal

A hearty chickpea stew with Mediterranean spices, tomatoes, and a hint of citrus.

Ingredients:

- 2 cans (14 oz each) chickpeas, drained
- 1 can (14 oz) diced tomatoes
- 1/2 cup red onion, finely chopped
- 2 cloves garlic, minced
- 2 carrots, sliced
- 1/2 cup celery, chopped
- 1 tsp ground cumin
- 1/2 tsp ground coriander
- 1/2 tsp paprika
- 1/4 tsp ground cinnamon
- Juice of 1 lemon
- Zest of 1 lemon
- Olive oil for cooking
- Salt and pepper to taste

Directions

1. In a large pot, sauté onion and garlic in olive oil until soft.
2. Add chickpeas, diced tomatoes, carrots, celery, ground cumin, ground coriander, paprika, ground cinnamon, salt, and pepper.
3. Simmer for 20 min until vegetables are tender.
4. Stir in lemon juice and lemon zest.
5. Serve hot.

Substitutions

- Add spinach for greens

4
servings

350

45 min

Normal

Vegan Spanish Paella

Ingredients:

- 1 1/2 cups Arborio rice
- 3 cups vegetable broth
- 1/2 cup bell peppers, diced
- 1/2 cup peas
- 1/2 cup artichoke hearts, sliced
- 1/4 cup red onion, finely chopped
- 2 cloves garlic, minced
- 1/2 tsp saffron threads (crushed and steeped in 2 tbsp warm water)
- 1/2 tsp paprika
- 1/4 tsp turmeric
- 1/4 cup cherry tomatoes, halved
- 2 tbsp olive oil
- Salt and pepper to taste

Substitutions

- Use vegetable paella seasoning

A colorful and flavorful Spanish paella featuring saffron-infused rice, vegetables, and plant-based protein.

Directions

1. In a large skillet, sauté onion and garlic in olive oil until soft.
2. Add Arborio rice, saffron-infused water, paprika, turmeric, salt, and pepper. Stir for 2 min.
3. Pour in vegetable broth and bring to a simmer.
4. Add bell peppers, peas, artichoke hearts, and cherry tomatoes.
5. Cover and cook for 20-25 min until rice is tender and liquid is absorbed.
6. Serve hot.

6 servings **320** **50 min**

Vegan Greek Spinach Pie

Ingredients:

- 12 sheets phyllo dough
- 10 cups fresh spinach
- 1/2 block firm tofu, crumbled
- 1/4 cup nutritional yeast
- 1/4 cup red onion, finely chopped
- 2 cloves garlic, minced
- 2 tbsp fresh dill, chopped
- 2 tbsp fresh parsley, chopped
- 3 tbsp olive oil
- Salt and pepper to taste

Substitutions

- Use kale instead of spinach

A savory spinach pie with layers of phyllo dough, spinach, tofu, and herbs.

Directions

1. Preheat oven to 375°F (190°C).
2. In a large skillet, sauté spinach until wilted. Drain excess liquid.
3. In a bowl, combine tofu, nutritional yeast, onion, garlic, dill, parsley, olive oil, salt, and pepper.
4. Lay one sheet of phyllo dough flat and brush with olive oil. Add another sheet on top and repeat.
5. Repeat the process until you have six layers.
6. Spread half of the spinach on top of the phyllo dough layers.
7. Add another layer of phyllo dough and brush with olive oil.
8. Add the remaining spinach on top.
9. Finish with a final layer of phyllo dough, brushing each sheet with olive oil.
10. Bake for 30 min until golden brown and crispy.
11. Serve hot or at room temperature.

4
servings

340

40 min

Vegan Italian Risotto with Roasted Vegetables

Ingredients:

- 1 1/2 cups Arborio rice
- 4 cups vegetable broth
- 1/2 cup white wine
- 2 cups mixed roasted vegetables (e.g., bell peppers, zucchini, cherry tomatoes)
- 1/2 cup red onion, finely chopped
- 2 cloves garlic, minced
- 2 tbsp olive oil
- 1/4 cup fresh basil, chopped
- Salt and pepper to taste

Substitutions

- Use vegetable stock instead of broth

Normal

Creamy Italian risotto infused with the flavors of roasted vegetables and a hint of white wine.

Directions

1. Preheat oven to 400°F (200°C).
2. Toss mixed vegetables with olive oil, salt, and pepper. Roast for 20 min.
3. In a large skillet, sauté onion and garlic in olive oil until soft.
4. Add Arborio rice and stir for 2 min.
5. Pour in white wine and cook until mostly absorbed.
6. Gradually add vegetable broth, stirring frequently until rice is creamy and tender (about 20 min).
7. Stir in roasted vegetables and fresh basil.
8. Serve hot.

4
servings

300

45 min

Normal

Vegan Turkish Eggplant and Lentil Stew

Ingredients:

- 2 eggplants, diced
- 1 cup green lentils, rinsed
- 1 can (14 oz) diced tomatoes
- 1/2 cup red onion, finely chopped
- 2 cloves garlic, minced
- 2 tbsp olive oil
- 2 tsp ground cumin
- 1 tsp ground coriander
- 1/2 tsp smoked paprika
- 1/4 tsp cayenne pepper
- Salt and pepper to taste
- Fresh pita bread for serving

Substitutions

- Add red bell peppers for extra flavor

A comforting Turkish stew with eggplant, lentils, and warming spices, served with pita bread.

Directions

1. In a large pot, sauté onion and garlic in olive oil until soft.
2. Add diced eggplant, lentils, diced tomatoes, ground cumin, ground coriander, smoked paprika, cayenne pepper, salt, and pepper.
3. Pour in enough water to cover the ingredients.
4. Simmer for 25-30 min until lentils are tender and the stew has thickened.
5. Serve hot with fresh pita bread.

Chapter 4
Mediterranean Bowls

2
servings

350

25 min

Vegan Mediterranean Quinoa Bowl

Ingredients:

- 1 cup cooked quinoa
- 1 cup roasted mixed vegetables (e.g., bell peppers, zucchini, cherry tomatoes)
- 1/2 cup chickpeas, cooked
- 1/4 cup Kalamata olives, sliced
- 1/4 cup red onion, finely chopped
- 2 tbsp fresh parsley, chopped
- 2 tbsp tahini
- 2 tbsp lemon juice
- 1 clove garlic, minced
- 2 tbsp olive oil
- Salt and pepper to taste

Substitutions

- Use couscous instead of quinoa

Easy

A nourishing bowl featuring quinoa, roasted vegetables, chickpeas, and a lemon-tahini dressing.

Directions

1. In a bowl, combine cooked quinoa, roasted vegetables, chickpeas, olives, onion, and parsley.
2. In a separate bowl, whisk together tahini, lemon juice, garlic, olive oil, salt, and pepper.
3. Drizzle dressing over the bowl.
4. Toss gently and serve.

2 servings

320

20 min

Vegan Greek Bowl with Tzatziki

Normal

A Greek-inspired bowl with falafel, tabbouleh salad, cucumber, tomato, and homemade tzatziki sauce.

Ingredients:

- 8 falafel patties (store-bought or homemade)
- 1 cup tabbouleh salad (store-bought or homemade)
- 1/2 cup cucumber, sliced
- 1/2 cup cherry tomatoes, halved
- 1/4 cup red onion, thinly sliced
- 1/4 cup Kalamata olives, sliced
- 1/4 cup fresh parsley, chopped
- 1/4 cup vegan tzatziki sauce (store-bought or homemade)
- Olive oil for frying (if making homemade falafel)
- Salt and pepper to taste

Substitutions

- Use store-bought falafel

Directions

1. If making homemade falafel, heat olive oil in a pan. Fry falafel patties until golden brown.
2. In a bowl, combine tabbouleh salad, cucumber, tomatoes, onion, olives, and parsley.
3. Warm falafel patties.
4. In a serving bowl, assemble the bowl by placing falafel in the center and arranging the tabbouleh salad, cucumber, and cherry tomatoes around it.
5. Drizzle with tzatziki sauce.
6. Garnish with fresh parsley.
7. Serve and enjoy!

2 servings   **320**   **20 min**

Vegan Moroccan Couscous Bowl

Easy

A Moroccan-inspired bowl with fluffy couscous, spiced chickpeas, roasted vegetables, and a harissa dressing.

Ingredients:

- 1 cup cooked couscous
- 1 cup spiced chickpeas (canned or homemade)
- 1 cup roasted mixed vegetables (e.g., bell peppers, carrots, zucchini)
- 1/4 cup red onion, finely chopped
- 2 tbsp fresh cilantro, chopped
- 2 tbsp harissa dressing (store-bought or homemade)
- Olive oil for roasting vegetables (if making from scratch)
- Salt and pepper to taste

Directions

1. In a bowl, combine cooked couscous, spiced chickpeas, roasted vegetables, onion, and cilantro.
2. Drizzle with harissa dressing.
3. Toss gently to coat.
4. Serve and enjoy the Moroccan flavors!

Substitutions

- Use quinoa instead of couscous

2
servings

380

25 min

Easy

Vegan Italian Pasta Bowl

mmmmmmm

Ingredients:

- 2 cups whole-grain pasta, cooked
- 1 cup marinara sauce (store-bought or homemade)
- 1 cup mixed sautéed vegetables (e.g., bell peppers, mushrooms, spinach)
- 1/4 cup red onion, finely chopped
- 2 cloves garlic, minced
- 1/4 cup vegan Parmesan cheese
- Fresh basil for garnish
- Olive oil for sautéing
- Salt and pepper to taste

Substitutions

- Use gluten-free pasta

An Italian-inspired bowl with whole-grain pasta, marinara sauce, sautéed vegetables, and vegan Parmesan.

Directions

1. In a skillet, sauté onion and garlic in olive oil until soft.
2. Add sautéed vegetables and cooked pasta. Cook for 2-3 min.
3. Pour in marinara sauce and heat until warmed through.
4. Season with salt and pepper.
5. Serve pasta in bowls, garnished with vegan Parmesan and fresh basil.
6. Enjoy the Italian flavors!

2
servings

380

30 min

Vegan Mediterranean Power Bowl

Ingredients:

- 1 cup cooked quinoa
- 2 cups kale, chopped
- 1 cup roasted sweet potatoes, diced
- 1/2 cup chickpeas, cooked
- 1/4 cup red onion, finely chopped
- 2 tbsp tahini
- 2 tbsp lemon juice
- 1 clove garlic, minced
- 2 tbsp olive oil
- Salt and pepper to taste

Easy

A powerhouse of a bowl with quinoa, kale, chickpeas, roasted sweet potatoes, and a lemon-tahini dressing.

Directions

1. In a bowl, combine cooked quinoa, chopped kale, roasted sweet potatoes, chickpeas, and red onion.
2. In a separate bowl, whisk together tahini, lemon juice, garlic, olive oil, salt, and pepper.
3. Drizzle dressing over the bowl.
4. Toss gently and serve.

Substitutions

- Use spinach instead of kale

2
servings

360

30 min

Normal

Vegan Falafel Bowl with Tahini Dressing

A falafel lover's dream bowl with crispy falafel, quinoa, cucumber, tomato, and a creamy tahini dressing.

Ingredients:

- 8 falafel patties (store-bought or homemade)
- 1 cup cooked quinoa
- 1/2 cup cucumber, sliced
- 1/2 cup cherry tomatoes, halved
- 1/4 cup red onion, thinly sliced
- 1/4 cup Kalamata olives, sliced
- 1/4 cup fresh parsley, chopped
- 1/4 cup tahini
- 2 tbsp lemon juice
- 1 clove garlic, minced
- 2 tbsp olive oil
- Salt and pepper to taste

Directions

1. If making homemade falafel, heat olive oil in a pan. Fry falafel patties until golden brown.
2. In a bowl, combine cooked quinoa, cucumber, tomatoes, onion, olives, and parsley.
3. Warm falafel patties.
4. In a serving bowl, assemble the bowl by placing falafel in the center and arranging the quinoa, cucumber, and cherry tomatoes around it.
5. Drizzle with tahini dressing.
6. Garnish with fresh parsley.
7. Serve and enjoy the falafel goodness!

Substitutions

- Use store-bought falafel

2
servings

280

25 min

Vegan Lebanese Mezze Platter

Ingredients:

- 1/2 cup hummus (store-bought or homemade)
- 1/2 cup baba ghanoush (store-bought or homemade)
- 8 falafel patties (store-bought or homemade)
- 1/4 cup Kalamata olives, sliced
- 1/4 cup cherry tomatoes, halved
- Fresh pita bread
- Olive oil for frying (if making homemade falafel)
- Fresh parsley for garnish

A delightful Lebanese mezze platter featuring hummus, baba ghanoush, falafel, olives, and pita bread.

Directions

1. If making homemade falafel, heat olive oil in a pan. Fry falafel patties until golden brown.
2. Arrange hummus, baba ghanoush, falafel, olives, and cherry tomatoes on a platter.
3. Warm pita bread.
4. Garnish with fresh parsley.
5. Serve the Lebanese mezze platter with pita bread for dipping and scooping.
6. Enjoy the flavors of Lebanon!

Substitutions

- Use store-bought pita bread

2 servings

350

25 min

Vegan Spanish Rice Bowl

Ingredients:

- 1 cup cooked saffron-infused rice
- 1 cup black beans, cooked
- 1 cup roasted bell peppers, sliced
- 1/4 cup red onion, finely chopped
- 2 cloves garlic, minced
- 1/4 cup fresh cilantro, chopped
- 1/4 cup tomato salsa (store-bought or homemade)
- Olive oil for roasting peppers (if making from scratch)
- Salt and pepper to taste

Easy

A vibrant Spanish rice bowl with saffron-infused rice, black beans, roasted peppers, and a tomato salsa.

Directions

1. In a bowl, combine cooked saffron-infused rice, black beans, roasted bell peppers, onion, and cilantro.
2. Drizzle with tomato salsa.
3. Toss gently to mix.
4. Serve and savor the flavors of Spain!

Substitutions

- Use white rice instead of saffron-infused rice

2
servings

280

20 min

Vegan Greek
Salad Bowl

A refreshing Greek salad bowl with lettuce, cucumber, cherry tomatoes, Kalamata olives, tofu feta, and Greek dressing.

Ingredients:

- 4 cups lettuce, chopped
- 1 cup cucumber, sliced
- 1 cup cherry tomatoes, halved
- 1/4 cup Kalamata olives, sliced
- 1/4 cup red onion, thinly sliced
- 1/2 cup tofu feta (store-bought or homemade)
- 1/4 cup Greek dressing (store-bought or homemade)
- Fresh oregano for garnish
- Olive oil (if making homemade tofu feta)
- Salt and pepper to taste

Directions

1. In a large bowl, combine lettuce, cucumber, cherry tomatoes, olives, and onion.
2. Add tofu feta on top.
3. Drizzle with Greek dressing.
4. Garnish with fresh oregano.
5. Season with salt and pepper.
6. Serve the Greek salad bowl and relish the Mediterranean flavors!

Substitutions

- Use store-bought tofu feta

2
servings

320

30 min

Easy

Vegan Italian Polenta Bowl

A comforting Italian bowl with creamy polenta, sautéed mushrooms, spinach, and a tomato-basil sauce.

Ingredients:

- 1 cup cooked polenta
- 1 cup sautéed mushrooms
- 1 cup sautéed spinach
- 1/4 cup tomato-basil sauce (store-bought or homemade)
- 1/4 cup vegan Parmesan cheese
- Fresh basil for garnish
- Olive oil for sautéing
- Salt and pepper to taste

Directions

1. In a skillet, sauté mushrooms in olive oil until tender. Set aside.
2. In the same skillet, sauté spinach until wilted. Set aside.
3. Reheat cooked polenta.
4. In a bowl, assemble the bowl by placing polenta in the center and arranging sautéed mushrooms and spinach around it.
5. Drizzle with tomato-basil sauce.
6. Garnish with vegan Parmesan and fresh basil.
7. Serve and enjoy the Italian comfort!

Substitutions

- Use vegan mozzarella cheese

Chapter 5
Mediterranean Wraps and Sandwiches

2 servings

320

15 min

Vegan Mediterranean Veggie Wrap

Easy

A veggie-packed Mediterranean wrap with hummus, roasted vegetables, and fresh herbs.

Ingredients:

- 2 large whole-grain wraps
- 1/2 cup hummus (store-bought or homemade)
- 1 cup roasted mixed vegetables (e.g., bell peppers, zucchini, eggplant)
- 1/2 cup cucumber, sliced
- 1/2 cup cherry tomatoes, halved
- 1/4 cup red onion, thinly sliced
- 1/4 cup fresh parsley, chopped
- Olive oil for roasting vegetables (if making from scratch)
- Salt and pepper to taste

Directions

1. If making from scratch, preheat oven to 425°F (220°C).
2. Toss mixed vegetables with olive oil, salt, and pepper. Roast for 20 min.
3. Warm whole-grain wraps.
4. Spread hummus on each wrap.
5. Place roasted vegetables, cucumber, tomatoes, onion, and parsley on top of the hummus.
6. Fold the sides of the wrap and roll it up.
7. Slice in half and serve.

Substitutions

- Use store-bought roasted vegetables

2
servings

340

20 min

Normal

Vegan Greek Gyro Wrap

Ingredients:

- 2 large whole-grain wraps
- 1 cup seitan or tofu gyro slices (store-bought or homemade)
- 1/4 cup tzatziki sauce (store-bought or homemade)
- 1/2 cup lettuce, shredded
- 1/2 cup cucumber, sliced
- 1/2 cup cherry tomatoes, halved
- 1/4 cup red onion, thinly sliced
- Olive oil for sautéing (if making homemade gyro slices)
- Salt and pepper to taste

A Greek gyro-inspired wrap with seitan or tofu gyro slices, tzatziki sauce, and fresh veggies.

Directions

1. If making homemade gyro slices, sauté seitan or tofu slices in olive oil until browned.
2. Warm whole-grain wraps.
3. Spread tzatziki sauce on each wrap.
4. Place gyro slices, lettuce, cucumber, tomatoes, onion, on top of the tzatziki sauce.
5. Roll up the wrap, securing the sides.
6. Slice in half and serve.

Substitutions

- Use store-bought gyro slices

2 servings

360

25 min

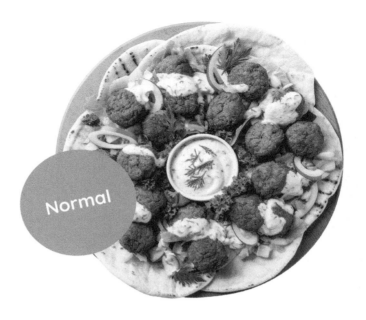

Vegan Falafel Pita with Tzatziki

A classic falafel pita with crispy falafel patties, homemade tzatziki sauce, and fresh veggies.

Ingredients:

- 2 large whole-grain pitas
- 8 falafel patties (store-bought or homemade)
- 1/2 cup tzatziki sauce (store-bought or homemade)
- 1/2 cup lettuce, shredded
- 1/2 cup cucumber, sliced
- 1/2 cup cherry tomatoes, halved
- 1/4 cup red onion, thinly sliced
- Olive oil for frying (if making homemade falafel)
- Salt and pepper to taste

Directions

1. If making homemade falafel, heat olive oil in a pan. Fry falafel patties until golden brown.
2. Warm whole-grain pitas.
3. Spread tzatziki sauce inside each pita.
4. Place falafel patties, lettuce, cucumber, tomatoes, and onion inside the pitas.
5. Serve and enjoy the falafel pita!

Substitutions

- Use store-bought falafel

2
servings

380

20 min

Vegan Italian Panini

Ingredients:

- 2 whole-grain ciabatta rolls
- 1 cup roasted mixed vegetables (e.g., bell peppers, zucchini, eggplant)
- 1/2 cup vegan mozzarella cheese, sliced
- 1/4 cup fresh basil leaves
- 2 tbsp basil pesto (store-bought or homemade)
- Olive oil for roasting vegetables (if making from scratch)
- Salt and pepper to taste

Substitutions

- Use store-bought roasted vegetables

A mouthwatering Italian panini with roasted vegetables, vegan mozzarella, and basil pesto.

Directions

1. If making from scratch, preheat oven to 425°F (220°C).
2. Toss mixed vegetables with olive oil, salt, and pepper. Roast for 20 min.
3. Cut ciabatta rolls in half.
4. Spread basil pesto on the bottom halves of the rolls.
5. Layer roasted vegetables, vegan mozzarella, and fresh basil on top of the pesto.
6. Place the top halves of the rolls on the fillings.
7. Heat a panini press or grill pan.
8. Grill the panini until the bread is crispy and the cheese is melted.
9. Slice and serve.

2
servings

340

25 min

Vegan Moroccan Spiced Wrap

Normal

A Moroccan-spiced wrap with chickpea patties, harissa sauce, and a colorful salad.

Ingredients:

- 2 large whole-grain wraps
- 8 chickpea patties (store-bought or homemade)
- 2 tbsp harissa sauce (store-bought or homemade)
- 1/2 cup lettuce, shredded
- 1/2 cup cucumber, sliced
- 1/2 cup cherry tomatoes, halved
- 1/4 cup red onion, thinly sliced
- 1/4 cup fresh cilantro, chopped
- Olive oil for frying (if making homemade chickpea patties)
- Salt and pepper to taste

Directions

1. If making homemade chickpea patties, heat olive oil in a pan. Fry chickpea patties until golden brown.
2. Warm whole-grain wraps.
3. Spread harissa sauce on each wrap.
4. Place chickpea patties, lettuce, cucumber, tomatoes, onion, and cilantro on top of the harissa sauce.
5. Roll up the wrap, securing the sides.
6. Slice in half and serve.

Substitutions

- Use store-bought chickpea patties

2
servings

360

30 min

Vegan Lebanese Shawarma

Ingredients:

- 2 large whole-grain wraps
- 1 cup marinated seitan or tofu shawarma slices (store-bought or homemade)
- 1/4 cup garlic sauce (store-bought or homemade)
- 1/2 cup pickled vegetables (e.g., cucumbers, carrots, turnips)
- 1/4 cup fresh parsley, chopped
- Olive oil for sautéing (if making homemade shawarma slices)
- Salt and pepper to taste

Substitutions

- Use store-bought shawarma slices

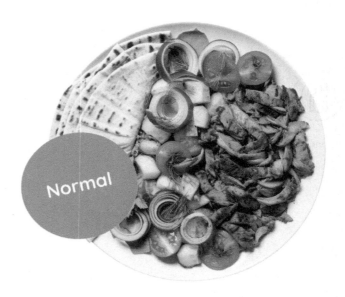

Normal

A Lebanese shawarma wrap with marinated seitan or tofu, garlic sauce, and pickled veggies.

Directions

1. If making homemade shawarma slices, sauté seitan or tofu slices in olive oil until browned.
2. Warm whole-grain wraps.
3. Spread garlic sauce on each wrap.
4. Place shawarma slices, pickled vegetables, and fresh parsley on top of the sauce.
5. Roll up the wrap, securing the sides.
6. Slice in half and serve.

2
servings

320

30 min

Easy

Vegan Spanish Tortilla Sandwich

Ingredients:

- 2 whole-grain baguettes or rolls
- 4 slices of Spanish tortilla (store-bought or homemade)
- 1/2 cup lettuce, shredded
- 1/2 cup tomato, sliced
- 1/4 cup red onion, thinly sliced
- Olive oil for cooking (if making homemade tortilla)
- Salt and pepper to taste

A Spanish-inspired tortilla sandwich with a fluffy potato omelette, lettuce, and tomato.

Directions

1. If making homemade tortilla, heat olive oil in a pan. Cook potato omelette until golden and set.
2. Slice the Spanish tortilla into sandwich-sized portions.
3. Cut the baguettes or rolls in half.
4. Layer lettuce, tomato, onion, and a slice of Spanish tortilla inside each baguette.
5. Season with salt and pepper.
6. Serve the Spanish tortilla sandwiches.

Substitutions

- Use store-bought Spanish tortilla

2
servings

340

25 min

Vegan Greek
Souvlaki Wrap

Ingredients:

- 2 large whole-grain wraps
- 1 cup marinated tempeh or tofu souvlaki (store-bought or homemade)
- 1/4 cup Greek dressing (store-bought or homemade)
- 1/2 cup lettuce, shredded
- 1/2 cup cucumber, sliced
- 1/2 cup cherry tomatoes, halved
- 1/4 cup red onion, thinly sliced
- Olive oil for sautéing (if making homemade souvlaki)
- Salt and pepper to taste

Normal

A Greek souvlaki wrap with marinated tempeh or tofu, Greek dressing, and fresh veggies.

Directions

1. If making homemade souvlaki, sauté tempeh or tofu slices in olive oil until browned.
2. Warm whole-grain wraps.
3. Spread Greek dressing on each wrap.
4. Place souvlaki slices, lettuce, cucumber, tomatoes, and onion on top of the dressing.
5. Roll up the wrap, securing the sides.
6. Slice in half and serve.

Substitutions

- Use store-bought souvlaki slices

2
servings

340

15 min

Vegan Italian Caprese Sandwich

Easy

A simple Italian Caprese sandwich with tomato, vegan mozzarella, fresh basil, and balsamic glaze.

Ingredients:

- 2 whole-grain ciabatta rolls
- 4 slices of vegan mozzarella cheese
- 1 cup tomato, sliced
- 1/2 cup fresh basil leaves
- 2 tbsp balsamic glaze (store-bought or homemade)
- Olive oil for drizzling
- Salt and pepper to taste

Directions

1. Cut ciabatta rolls in half.
2. Layer slices of vegan mozzarella, tomato, and fresh basil on the bottom halves of the rolls.
3. Drizzle with balsamic glaze, olive oil, salt, and pepper.
4. Place the top halves of the rolls on the fillings.
5. Serve the Italian Caprese sandwiches.

Substitutions

- Use store-bought vegan mozzarella

2
servings

360

30 min

Vegan Turkish Kebab Wrap

Ingredients:

- 2 large whole-grain wraps
- 1 cup spiced seitan or tofu kebab slices (store-bought or homemade)
- 1/4 cup tahini sauce (store-bought or homemade)
- 1/2 cup lettuce, shredded
- 1/2 cup cucumber, sliced
- 1/2 cup cherry tomatoes, halved
- 1/4 cup red onion, thinly sliced
- Olive oil for sautéing (if making homemade kebab slices)
- Salt and pepper to taste

Substitutions

- Use store-bought kebab slices

Normal

A Turkish kebab wrap with spiced seitan or tofu, tahini sauce, and a colorful salad.

Directions

1. If making homemade kebab slices, sauté seitan or tofu slices in olive oil until browned.
2. Warm whole-grain wraps.
3. Spread tahini sauce on each wrap.
4. Place kebab slices, lettuce, cucumber, tomatoes, and onion on top of the sauce.
5. Roll up the wrap, securing the sides.
6. Slice in half and serve.

We have a small favor to ask

My dear fellow food enthusiasts and fans of Mediterranean flavors,

I hope the journey through these pages of the "Mediterranean Plant-Based Cookbook: From Olive Grove to Table" has been as delightful for you as it has been for me. The Mediterranean region, with its rich culinary heritage, is a treasure trove of wholesome, plant-based dishes. From the sun-kissed olive groves to the vibrant dining tables, the flavors are nothing short of a celebration of life itself.

I'd like to take a moment to talk about something that's very close to our hearts. You see, for small publishers like us, reviews are akin to the secret ingredients that make a dish extraordinary. They are the essence of our creative spirit and the lifeblood of our work.

I want to emphasize that your reviews, regardless of their length or the number of stars they bear, are of immense value to us. Each one is a testament to the beautiful journey we embarked on when we decided to create this cookbook. Every single review is like a star in the night sky, guiding others to the treasures of the Mediterranean table we've shared.

So, if you've experienced the magic of Mediterranean cuisine through these recipes, if you've been transported to a seaside taverna or a family dinner in a quaint village, if the flavors have brought you comfort and joy, then I kindly ask for your assistance. Please take a moment to return to the platform or app where you acquired this book. There, you'll find the review button waiting for your feedback.

A simple star rating accompanied by a brief sentence sharing your thoughts can have a profound impact, much like the fusion of flavors in a perfect mezze platter. Your reviews can inspire others to embark on this culinary journey and discover the bountiful and wholesome world of Mediterranean plant-based dishes.

As we conclude this moment of reflection, let's return to what truly unites us: the love for Mediterranean cuisine. Now, with your support, may these recipes continue to be a source of inspiration, flavor, and togetherness for generations to come.

Thank you for being an essential part of our culinary voyage, and here's to the boundless joys of Mediterranean plant-based cooking.

With warmest regards,

Chapter 6
Mediterranean Salads

2 servings

280

15 min

Easy

Vegan Greek Salad

〜〜〜〜〜〜〜〜〜

Ingredients:

- 4 cups lettuce, chopped
- 1 cup cucumber, sliced
- 1 cup cherry tomatoes, halved
- 1/4 cup Kalamata olives, sliced
- 1/4 cup red onion, thinly sliced
- 1/2 cup vegan feta cheese, crumbled (store-bought or homemade)
- 1/4 cup Greek dressing (store-bought or homemade)
- Fresh oregano for garnish
- Olive oil (if making homemade vegan feta)
- Salt and pepper to taste

Substitutions

- Use store-bought vegan feta

A classic Greek salad with crisp lettuce, cucumber, cherry tomatoes, Kalamata olives, and vegan feta.

Directions

1. If making homemade vegan feta, combine crumbled tofu, lemon juice, olive oil, garlic powder, nutritional yeast, salt, and pepper. Refrigerate to marinate.
2. In a large bowl, combine lettuce, cucumber, cherry tomatoes, olives, and onion.
3. Add vegan feta on top.
4. Drizzle with Greek dressing.
5. Garnish with fresh oregano.
6. Season with salt and pepper.
7. Serve the Greek salad and enjoy!

2
servings

320

15 min

Easy

Vegan Mediterranean Chickpea Salad

Ingredients:

- 2 cups cooked chickpeas
- 1 cup cucumber, diced
- 1 cup cherry tomatoes, halved
- 1/4 cup red onion, finely chopped
- 2 tbsp fresh parsley, chopped
- 2 tbsp tahini
- 2 tbsp lemon juice
- 1 clove garlic, minced
- 2 tbsp olive oil
- Salt and pepper to taste

A hearty Mediterranean chickpea salad with chickpeas, cucumbers, cherry tomatoes, and a lemon-tahini dressing.

Directions

1. In a bowl, combine cooked chickpeas, cucumber, cherry tomatoes, onion, and parsley.
2. In a separate bowl, whisk together tahini, lemon juice, garlic, olive oil, salt, and pepper.
3. Drizzle dressing over the salad.
4. Toss gently and serve.

Substitutions

- Use canned chickpeas

2
servings

340

20 min

Easy

Vegan Moroccan Couscous Salad

A Moroccan-inspired couscous salad with fluffy couscous, spiced chickpeas, dried fruits, and nuts.

Ingredients:

- 1 cup cooked couscous
- 1 cup spiced chickpeas (canned or homemade)
- 1/4 cup dried apricots, chopped
- 1/4 cup dried cranberries
- 1/4 cup slivered almonds
- 1/4 cup fresh cilantro, chopped
- 2 tbsp lemon juice
- 2 tbsp olive oil
- 1/2 tsp ground cumin
- 1/2 tsp ground coriander
- Salt and pepper to taste

Directions

1. In a bowl, combine cooked couscous, spiced chickpeas, dried apricots, dried cranberries, almonds, and cilantro.
2. In a separate bowl, whisk together lemon juice, olive oil, ground cumin, ground coriander, salt, and pepper.
3. Drizzle dressing over the salad.
4. Toss gently to combine.
5. Serve and savor the Moroccan flavors!

Substitutions

- Use quinoa instead of couscous

2 servings

280

15 min

Easy

Vegan Italian Caprese Salad

~~~~~~~~~~~~

Ingredients:

- 2 cups cherry tomatoes, halved
- 1 cup vegan mozzarella cheese, cubed
- 1/2 cup fresh basil leaves
- 2 tbsp balsamic glaze (store-bought or homemade)
- Olive oil for drizzling
- Salt and pepper to taste

A simple Italian Caprese salad with tomato, vegan mozzarella, fresh basil, and balsamic glaze.

Directions

1. In a bowl, combine cherry tomatoes, vegan mozzarella cheese, and fresh basil leaves.
2. Drizzle with balsamic glaze and olive oil.
3. Season with salt and pepper.
4. Toss gently to mix.
5. Serve the Italian Caprese salad and enjoy!

Substitutions

- Use store-bought vegan mozzarella

**2
servings**

280

20 min

Vegan Lebanese Tabbouleh

Ingredients:

- 1 cup cooked bulgur
- 1 cup fresh parsley, finely chopped
- 1/2 cup cherry tomatoes, diced
- 1/2 cup cucumber, diced
- 1/4 cup red onion, finely chopped
- 2 tbsp fresh mint, chopped
- 2 tbsp lemon juice
- 2 tbsp olive oil
- Salt and pepper to taste

Easy

A refreshing Lebanese tabbouleh salad with finely chopped parsley, tomatoes, cucumbers, and bulgur.

Directions

1. In a bowl, combine cooked bulgur, finely chopped parsley, diced tomatoes, diced cucumber, onion, and fresh mint.
2. In a separate bowl, whisk together lemon juice, olive oil, salt, and pepper.
3. Drizzle dressing over the tabbouleh salad.
4. Toss gently and serve.

Substitutions

- Use quinoa instead of bulgur

2
servings

250

15 min

Easy

Vegan Spanish Gazpacho

Ingredients:

- 4 ripe tomatoes, diced
- 1 cucumber, peeled and diced
- 1 red bell pepper, diced
- 1/4 cup red onion, finely chopped
- 2 cloves garlic, minced
- 2 tbsp olive oil
- 2 tbsp red wine vinegar
- 1 tsp paprika
- Salt and pepper to taste

A chilled Spanish gazpacho soup made with ripe tomatoes, cucumber, bell pepper, and garlic.

Directions

1. In a blender, combine diced tomatoes, cucumber, red bell pepper, onion, garlic, olive oil, red wine vinegar, paprika, salt, and pepper.
2. Blend until smooth.
3. Chill the gazpacho in the refrigerator for at least 1 hour.
4. Serve the chilled Spanish gazpacho soup.

Substitutions

- Add a dash of hot sauce for spice

2
servings

340

20 min

Easy

Vegan Greek Pasta Salad

Ingredients:

- 2 cups cooked pasta (e.g., penne)
- 1/4 cup Kalamata olives, sliced
- 1 cup cherry tomatoes, halved
- 1/4 cup red onion, thinly sliced
- 1/4 cup cucumber, diced
- 1/4 cup vegan feta cheese, crumbled (store-bought or homemade)
- 1/4 cup Greek dressing (store-bought or homemade)
- Fresh oregano for garnish
- Salt and pepper to taste

A delightful Greek pasta salad with cooked pasta, Kalamata olives, cherry tomatoes, and Greek dressing.

Directions

1. In a bowl, combine cooked pasta, Kalamata olives, cherry tomatoes, onion, cucumber, and vegan feta cheese.
2. Drizzle with Greek dressing.
3. Garnish with fresh oregano.
4. Season with salt and pepper.
5. Toss gently to mix.
6. Serve the Greek pasta salad and enjoy!

Substitutions

- Use store-bought vegan feta

2 servings

320 kcal

20 min

Easy

Vegan Italian Panzanella Salad

Ingredients:

- 2 cups stale crusty bread, torn into pieces
- 1 cup cherry tomatoes, halved
- 1 cup cucumber, sliced
- 1/2 cup red onion, thinly sliced
- 1/2 cup fresh basil leaves
- 2 tbsp red wine vinegar
- 2 tbsp olive oil
- Salt and pepper to taste

A Tuscan-inspired Italian panzanella salad with crusty bread, tomatoes, cucumber, and basil.

Directions

1. In a large bowl, combine torn bread pieces, cherry tomatoes, cucumber, onion, and fresh basil leaves.
2. In a separate bowl, whisk together red wine vinegar, olive oil, salt, and pepper.
3. Drizzle dressing over the panzanella salad.
4. Toss gently to mix.
5. Allow the salad to sit for 10 minutes to let the flavors meld.
6. Serve and enjoy the Italian panzanella salad!

Substitutions

- Use balsamic vinegar for variation

2
servings

280

20 min

Vegan Turkish Shepherd's Salad

Easy

A colorful Turkish shepherd's salad with diced vegetables, parsley, and a zesty lemon-olive oil dressing.

Ingredients:

- 1 cup cucumber, diced
- 1 cup tomato, diced
- 1/2 cup red bell pepper, diced
- 1/4 cup red onion, finely chopped
- 2 tbsp fresh parsley, chopped
- 2 tbsp lemon juice
- 2 tbsp olive oil
- Salt and pepper to taste

Directions

1. In a bowl, combine diced cucumber, diced tomato, diced red bell pepper, onion, and fresh parsley.
2. In a separate bowl, whisk together lemon juice, olive oil, salt, and pepper.
3. Drizzle dressing over the shepherd's salad.
4. Toss gently to mix.
5. Serve and enjoy the Turkish shepherd's salad!

Substitutions

- Add diced olives for extra flavor

2 servings   **320**   **25 min**

Easy

Vegan Mediterranean Potato Salad

mmmmmmm

Ingredients:

- 2 cups cooked and diced potatoes
- 1/4 cup Kalamata olives, sliced
- 1 cup cherry tomatoes, halved
- 1/4 cup red onion, finely chopped
- 1/4 cup fresh parsley, chopped
- 1/4 cup vegan mayonnaise
- 2 tbsp lemon juice
- 2 tbsp olive oil
- 1 tsp Dijon mustard
- Salt and pepper to taste

A creamy Mediterranean potato salad with tender potatoes, olives, cherry tomatoes, and a tangy dressing.

Directions

1. In a bowl, combine cooked and diced potatoes, Kalamata olives, cherry tomatoes, onion, and fresh parsley.
2. In a separate bowl, whisk together vegan mayonnaise, lemon juice, olive oil, Dijon mustard, salt, and pepper.
3. Drizzle dressing over the potato salad.
4. Toss gently to mix.
5. Serve the creamy Mediterranean potato salad and enjoy!

Substitutions

- Use store-bought vegan mayonnaise

Chapter 7
Mediterranean Soups and Stews

4
servings

240

30 min

Easy

Vegan Lentil Soup with Spinach

A comforting vegan lentil soup with hearty lentils, fresh spinach, and aromatic spices.

Ingredients:

- 1 cup brown lentils, rinsed and drained
- 1/2 cup onion, chopped
- 1/2 cup carrot, diced
- 1/2 cup celery, diced
- 3 cloves garlic, minced
- 1 tsp cumin
- 1/2 tsp paprika
- 1/2 tsp ground turmeric
- 1/4 tsp cayenne pepper (adjust to taste)
- 4 cups vegetable broth
- 2 cups water
- 2 cups fresh spinach, chopped
- 2 tbsp olive oil
- Salt and pepper to taste

Directions

1. In a large pot, heat olive oil over medium heat.
2. Add chopped onion, carrot, celery, and minced garlic. Sauté until softened.
3. Stir in cumin, paprika, ground turmeric, and cayenne pepper.
4. Add brown lentils, vegetable broth, and water. Bring to a boil.
5. Reduce heat, cover, and simmer for 20-25 minutes or until lentils are tender.
6. Stir in fresh spinach and cook until wilted.
7. Season with salt and pepper.
8. Serve the vegan lentil soup hot. Enjoy!

Substitutions

- Use green or red lentils

4 servings

280 kcal

40 min

Normal

Vegan Moroccan Harira Soup

A hearty Moroccan harira soup with chickpeas, lentils, tomatoes, and fragrant spices.

Ingredients:

- 1/2 cup brown lentils, rinsed and drained
- 1/2 cup chickpeas, cooked (canned or homemade)
- 1/2 cup onion, chopped
- 1/2 cup celery, chopped
- 1/2 cup carrot, chopped
- 3 cloves garlic, minced
- 1 tsp ground cumin
- 1 tsp ground coriander
- 1/2 tsp ground cinnamon
- 1/4 tsp ground turmeric
- 1/4 tsp cayenne pepper (adjust to taste)
- 1 can (14 oz) diced tomatoes
- 4 cups vegetable broth
- 2 tbsp fresh cilantro, chopped
- 2 tbsp fresh parsley, chopped
- 2 tbsp lemon juice
- 2 tbsp olive oil
- Salt and pepper to taste

Substitutions

- Use red lentils for a smoother soup texture

Directions

1. In a large pot, heat olive oil over medium heat.
2. Add chopped onion, celery, carrot, and minced garlic. Sauté until softened.
3. Stir in ground cumin, ground coriander, ground cinnamon, ground turmeric, and cayenne pepper.
4. Add brown lentils, chickpeas, diced tomatoes, and vegetable broth. Bring to a boil.
5. Reduce heat, cover, and simmer for 30 minutes or until lentils are tender.
6. Stir in fresh cilantro, fresh parsley, and lemon juice.
7. Season with salt and pepper.
8. Serve the Moroccan harira soup hot. Enjoy!

4
servings

250

35 min

Vegan Italian Minestrone Soup

Ingredients:

- 1/2 cup onion, chopped
- 1/2 cup carrot, diced
- 1/2 cup celery, diced
- 1/2 cup zucchini, diced
- 1/2 cup green beans, chopped
- 3 cloves garlic, minced
- 1 can (14 oz) diced tomatoes
- 1/2 cup small pasta (e.g., ditalini or small shells)
- 4 cups vegetable broth
- 1 tsp dried basil
- 1 tsp dried oregano
- 1/2 tsp dried thyme
- 1/2 tsp dried rosemary
- 1 bay leaf
- 2 tbsp olive oil
- Salt and pepper to taste

Substitutions

- Use any small pasta shapes

Easy

A classic Italian minestrone soup with a medley of vegetables, pasta, and flavorful herbs.

Directions

1. In a large pot, heat olive oil over medium heat.
2. Add chopped onion, carrot, celery, zucchini, green beans, and minced garlic. Sauté until softened.
3. Stir in diced tomatoes, vegetable broth, dried basil, dried oregano, dried thyme, dried rosemary, and bay leaf.
4. Bring to a boil, then reduce heat.
5. Add small pasta and simmer for 10-12 minutes or until pasta is tender.
6. Season with salt and pepper.
7. Remove the bay leaf before serving.
8. Serve the Italian minestrone soup hot. Enjoy!

4
servings

260

30 min

Vegan Lebanese Lentil Soup

Easy

A comforting Lebanese lentil soup with red lentils, vegetables, and a touch of lemon.

Ingredients:

- 1 cup red lentils, rinsed and drained
- 1/2 cup onion, chopped
- 1/2 cup carrot, diced
- 1/2 cup celery, diced
- 3 cloves garlic, minced
- 1 tsp ground cumin
- 1/2 tsp ground coriander
- 1/4 tsp ground turmeric
- 4 cups vegetable broth
- 2 cups water
- 2 tbsp lemon juice
- 2 tbsp olive oil
- Salt and pepper to taste

Substitutions

- Use brown or green lentils

Directions

1. In a large pot, heat olive oil over medium heat.
2. Add chopped onion, carrot, celery, and minced garlic. Sauté until softened.
3. Stir in ground cumin, ground coriander, ground turmeric, and red lentils.
4. Add vegetable broth and water. Bring to a boil.
5. Reduce heat, cover, and simmer for 20-25 minutes or until lentils are tender.
6. Stir in lemon juice.
7. Season with salt and pepper.
8. Serve the Lebanese lentil soup hot. Enjoy!

4 servings

280

25 min

Normal

Vegan Greek Avgolemono Soup

A creamy and tangy Greek Avgolemono soup with orzo, lemon, and a velvety broth.

Ingredients:

- 1/2 cup orzo pasta
- 4 cups vegetable broth
- 1/4 cup lemon juice
- 2 tsp lemon zest
- 2 cloves garlic, minced
- 2 tbsp olive oil
- 2 tbsp fresh dill, chopped
- 2 tbsp fresh parsley, chopped
- 2 tbsp cornstarch
- Salt and pepper to taste

Directions

1. In a pot, heat olive oil over medium heat.
2. Add minced garlic and sauté briefly until fragrant.
3. Add orzo pasta and stir until lightly toasted.
4. Pour in vegetable broth and bring to a boil.
5. Reduce heat and simmer for 10-12 minutes or until orzo is tender.
6. In a separate bowl, whisk together lemon juice, lemon zest, cornstarch, and a ladle of hot soup broth to make a slurry.
7. Slowly pour the slurry back into the soup, stirring continuously until it thickens.
8. Stir in fresh dill and fresh parsley.
9. Season with salt and pepper.
10. Serve the Greek Avgolemono soup hot. Enjoy!

Substitutions

- Use rice instead of orzo

4 servings

250

15 min

Easy

Vegan Spanish Gazpacho

Ingredients:

- 4 ripe tomatoes, diced
- 1 cucumber, peeled and diced
- 1 red bell pepper, diced
- 1/4 cup red onion, finely chopped
- 2 cloves garlic, minced
- 2 tbsp olive oil
- 2 tbsp red wine vinegar
- 1 tsp paprika
- Salt and pepper to taste

A chilled Spanish gazpacho soup made with ripe tomatoes, cucumber, bell pepper, and garlic.

Directions

1. In a blender, combine diced tomatoes, cucumber, red bell pepper, onion, garlic, olive oil, red wine vinegar, paprika, salt, and pepper.
2. Blend until smooth.
3. Chill the gazpacho in the refrigerator for at least 1 hour.
4. Serve the chilled Spanish gazpacho soup. Enjoy!

Substitutions

- Add a dash of hot sauce for spice

4 servings

320

35 min

Vegan Mediterranean Chickpea Stew

Normal

A hearty Mediterranean chickpea stew with chickpeas, vegetables, and Mediterranean spices.

Ingredients:

- 2 cans (15 oz each) chickpeas, rinsed and drained
- 1/2 cup onion, chopped
- 1/2 cup bell pepper (any color), diced
- 1/2 cup zucchini, diced
- 3 cloves garlic, minced
- 1 can (14 oz) diced tomatoes
- 1/4 cup fresh parsley, chopped
- 2 tsp ground cumin
- 1 tsp ground paprika
- 1/2 tsp ground coriander
- 1/2 tsp dried oregano
- 2 cups vegetable broth
- 2 tbsp olive oil
- Salt and pepper to taste

Substitutions

- Use diced eggplant for variety

Directions

1. In a large pot, heat olive oil over medium heat.
2. Add chopped onion, bell pepper, zucchini, and minced garlic. Sauté until softened.
3. Stir in ground cumin, ground paprika, ground coriander, dried oregano, and chickpeas.
4. Add diced tomatoes and vegetable broth. Bring to a simmer.
5. Cover and cook for 20-25 minutes, stirring occasionally.
6. Stir in fresh parsley.
7. Season with salt and pepper.
8. Serve the Mediterranean chickpea stew hot. Enjoy!

4 servings

260

30 min

Easy

Vegan Italian Tomato and Basil Soup

Ingredients:

- 1 can (14 oz) diced tomatoes
- 1/2 cup onion, chopped
- 1/2 cup celery, chopped
- 1/2 cup carrot, chopped
- 3 cloves garlic, minced
- 1 tsp dried basil
- 1/2 tsp dried oregano
- 1/4 tsp red pepper flakes (adjust to taste)
- 4 cups vegetable broth
- 2 tbsp fresh basil, chopped
- 2 tbsp olive oil
- Salt and pepper to taste

Substitutions

- Use canned whole tomatoes and crush them in the pot

A comforting Italian tomato and basil soup with rich tomato flavor and fragrant fresh basil.

Directions

1. In a large pot, heat olive oil over medium heat.
2. Add chopped onion, celery, carrot, and minced garlic. Sauté until softened.
3. Stir in diced tomatoes, dried basil, dried oregano, and red pepper flakes.
4. Add vegetable broth and bring to a simmer.
5. Cover and cook for 15-20 minutes.
6. Stir in fresh basil.
7. Season with salt and pepper.
8. Serve the Italian tomato and basil soup hot. Enjoy!

4 servings

270 kcal

35 min

Easy

Vegan Turkish Red Lentil Soup

A comforting Turkish red lentil soup with red lentils, vegetables, and warming spices.

Ingredients:

- 1 cup red lentils, rinsed and drained
- 1/2 cup onion, chopped
- 1/2 cup carrot, diced
- 1/2 cup red bell pepper, diced
- 3 cloves garlic, minced
- 1 tsp ground cumin
- 1/2 tsp ground paprika
- 1/2 tsp ground coriander
- 4 cups vegetable broth
- 2 tbsp fresh lemon juice
- 2 tbsp olive oil
- Salt and pepper to taste

Directions

1. In a large pot, heat olive oil over medium heat.
2. Add chopped onion, carrot, red bell pepper, and minced garlic. Sauté until softened.
3. Stir in ground cumin, ground paprika, ground coriander, and red lentils.
4. Add vegetable broth and bring to a boil.
5. Reduce heat, cover, and simmer for 20-25 minutes or until lentils are tender.
6. Stir in fresh lemon juice.
7. Season with salt and pepper.
8. Serve the Turkish red lentil soup hot. Enjoy!

Substitutions

- Use green or brown lentils

4
servings

320

45 min

Vegan Moroccan Chickpea Tagine

Normal

A Moroccan-inspired chickpea tagine with chickpeas, vegetables, dried fruits, and aromatic spices.

Ingredients:

- 2 cans (15 oz each) chickpeas, rinsed and drained
- 1/2 cup onion, chopped
- 1/2 cup bell pepper (any color), diced
- 1/2 cup eggplant, diced
- 1/2 cup zucchini, diced
- 1/4 cup dried apricots, chopped
- 1/4 cup dried cranberries
- 2 cloves garlic, minced
- 2 tsp ground cumin
- 1 tsp ground coriander
- 1/2 tsp ground cinnamon
- 1/2 tsp ground turmeric
- 2 cups vegetable broth
- 2 tbsp olive oil
- Salt and pepper to taste

Substitutions

- Use diced sweet potatoes for extra sweetness

Directions

1. In a large pot, heat olive oil over medium heat.
2. Add chopped onion, bell pepper, eggplant, zucchini, and minced garlic. Sauté until softened.
3. Stir in ground cumin, ground coriander, ground cinnamon, ground turmeric, and chickpeas.
4. Add dried apricots, dried cranberries, and vegetable broth. Bring to a simmer.
5. Cover and cook for 30-35 minutes, stirring occasionally.
6. Season with salt and pepper.
7. Serve the Moroccan chickpea tagine hot. Enjoy!

Chapter 8
Mediterranean Pasta Dishes

2 servings

350

15 min

Easy

Vegan Italian Spaghetti Aglio e Olio

A classic Italian spaghetti dish with simple ingredients: garlic, olive oil, red pepper flakes, and parsley.

Ingredients:

- 8 oz spaghetti
- 4 cloves garlic, thinly sliced
- 1/4 cup olive oil
- 1/2 tsp red pepper flakes (adjust to taste)
- 2 tbsp fresh parsley, chopped
- Salt to taste

Directions

1. Cook spaghetti according to package instructions until al dente. Drain and set aside.
2. In a skillet, heat olive oil over low heat.
3. Add thinly sliced garlic and red pepper flakes. Sauté gently until garlic is fragrant and just beginning to turn golden (about 2 minutes).
4. Toss in cooked spaghetti and stir to coat with garlic-infused oil.
5. Season with salt.
6. Sprinkle with fresh parsley.
7. Serve the vegan Italian spaghetti Aglio e Olio hot. Enjoy!

Substitutions

- Use whole wheat or gluten-free spaghetti

4 servings

400 kcal

60 min

Vegan Greek Pastitsio

A hearty Greek pastitsio with layers of pasta, vegan bechamel sauce, and a savory lentil-based filling.

Ingredients:

- 8 oz ziti or penne pasta, cooked
- 1 cup green or brown lentils, cooked
- 1/2 cup onion, chopped
- 2 cloves garlic, minced
- 1 can (14 oz) diced tomatoes
- 1 tsp dried oregano
- 1/2 tsp ground cinnamon
- 1/4 tsp ground nutmeg
- Salt and pepper to taste
- 1 tbsp olive oil
- Vegan bechamel sauce (store-bought or homemade)

Substitutions

- Use vegan ricotta or tofu-based ricotta for a creamier filling

Directions

1. In a large skillet, heat olive oil over medium heat.
2. Add chopped onion and minced garlic. Sauté until softened.
3. Stir in cooked lentils, diced tomatoes, dried oregano, ground cinnamon, ground nutmeg, salt, and pepper.
4. Simmer for 15-20 minutes, or until the mixture thickens.
5. Preheat the oven to 350°F (175°C).
6. In a greased baking dish, layer cooked pasta, lentil mixture, and a generous amount of vegan bechamel sauce.
7. Repeat the layers.
8. Bake for 25-30 minutes or until the top is golden brown.
9. Serve the vegan Greek pastitsio hot. Enjoy!

4 servings

320

30 min

Vegan Moroccan Couscous with Vegetables

Ingredients:

- 1 1/2 cups couscous
- 2 cups vegetable broth
- 1/2 cup butternut squash, diced
- 1/2 cup zucchini, diced
- 1/2 cup red bell pepper, diced
- 1/2 cup red onion, diced
- 1/4 cup dried apricots, chopped
- 1/4 cup dried cranberries
- 2 tbsp olive oil
- 1 tsp ground cumin
- 1/2 tsp ground coriander
- 1/2 tsp ground cinnamon
- 1/4 tsp ground turmeric
- Salt and pepper to taste

Substitutions

- Use quinoa instead of couscous

Easy

A flavorful Moroccan couscous dish with a medley of roasted vegetables, dried fruits, and aromatic spices.

Directions

1. Preheat the oven to 400°F (200°C).
2. In a large bowl, toss diced butternut squash, zucchini, red bell pepper, and red onion with olive oil, ground cumin, ground coriander, ground cinnamon, ground turmeric, salt, and pepper.
3. Spread the vegetables on a baking sheet and roast for 20-25 minutes, or until tender and slightly caramelized.
4. While the vegetables are roasting, prepare couscous by bringing vegetable broth to a boil in a saucepan. Stir in couscous, cover, and remove from heat. Let it sit for 5 minutes, then fluff with a fork.
5. In a large serving bowl, combine cooked couscous, roasted vegetables, dried apricots, and dried cranberries.
6. Toss to mix well.
7. Serve the vegan Moroccan couscous with vegetables hot. Enjoy!

4 servings

380 kcal

45 min

Vegan Italian Eggplant Parmesan

Normal

A vegan twist on the classic Italian eggplant Parmesan, featuring breaded and baked eggplant slices.

Ingredients:

- 2 large eggplants, sliced into 1/2-inch rounds
- 2 cups breadcrumbs (use vegan breadcrumbs)
- 1 cup marinara sauce (store-bought or homemade)
- 1 cup vegan mozzarella cheese, shredded
- 1/2 cup vegan Parmesan cheese
- 2 tbsp fresh basil, chopped
- 2 tbsp fresh parsley, chopped
- Olive oil for brushing
- Salt and pepper to taste

Substitutions

- Use store-bought vegan eggplant cutlets for a quicker version

Directions

1. Preheat the oven to 375°F (190°C).
2. Brush eggplant slices with olive oil and season with salt and pepper.
3. Dredge each eggplant slice in breadcrumbs, pressing to adhere.
4. Place breaded eggplant slices on a baking sheet and bake for 20-25 minutes, flipping halfway through, until golden brown.
5. In a greased baking dish, layer marinara sauce, baked eggplant slices, vegan mozzarella cheese, and vegan Parmesan cheese.
6. Repeat the layers.
7. Bake for an additional 20-25 minutes or until the cheese is bubbly and golden.
8. Garnish with chopped fresh basil and parsley.
9. Serve the vegan Italian eggplant Parmesan hot. Enjoy!

4
servings

320

35 min

Normal

Vegan Lebanese Tofu Kebabs with Tahini

Ingredients:

- 1 block (14 oz) extra-firm tofu, pressed and cubed
- 1/4 cup tahini
- 2 tbsp lemon juice
- 2 cloves garlic, minced
- 1 tsp ground cumin
- 1/2 tsp ground coriander
- 1/2 tsp smoked paprika
- 1/4 tsp cayenne pepper (adjust to taste)
- Salt and pepper to taste
- Wooden skewers, soaked in water

Substitutions

- Use tempeh or seitan for a different protein option

Flavorful Lebanese-style tofu kebabs marinated in Middle Eastern spices and served with tahini sauce.

Directions

1. In a bowl, prepare the marinade by combining tahini, lemon juice, minced garlic, ground cumin, ground coriander, smoked paprika, cayenne pepper, salt, and pepper.
2. Thread cubed tofu onto soaked wooden skewers.
3. Brush tofu skewers generously with the marinade.
4. Preheat a grill or grill pan over medium-high heat.
5. Grill tofu skewers for 2-3 minutes per side, or until grill marks appear and tofu is heated through.
6. Serve the Lebanese tofu kebabs hot with additional tahini sauce for dipping. Enjoy!

4 servings

380

45 min

Vegan Spanish Paella with Saffron

Normal

A classic Spanish paella loaded with saffron-infused rice, colorful vegetables, and plant-based proteins.

Ingredients:

- 1 1/2 cups Arborio rice
- 4 cups vegetable broth
- 1 cup cherry tomatoes, halved
- 1/2 cup bell pepper (any color), diced
- 1/2 cup green peas
- 1/2 cup artichoke hearts, quartered
- 1/2 cup cooked chickpeas (canned or homemade)
- 1/4 cup roasted red pepper strips
- 1/4 cup red onion, thinly sliced
- 3 cloves garlic, minced
- 1/4 tsp saffron threads (soaked in 2 tbsp warm water)
- 2 tbsp olive oil
- 1 tsp smoked paprika
- 1/2 tsp paprika
- Salt and pepper to taste

Substitutions

- Add plant-based sausage for extra flavor

Directions

1. In a large paella pan or skillet, heat olive oil over medium heat.
2. Add minced garlic and sliced red onion. Sauté until softened.
3. Stir in Arborio rice and cook for 2-3 minutes, stirring frequently.
4. Pour in vegetable broth and add soaked saffron threads with their water, smoked paprika, paprika, salt, and pepper.
5. Arrange cherry tomatoes, bell pepper, green peas, artichoke hearts, chickpeas, and roasted red pepper strips on top of the rice.
6. Cover and simmer for 20-25 minutes or until the rice is tender and the liquid is absorbed.
7. Remove from heat and let it rest for a few minutes.
8. Serve the vegan Spanish paella hot. Enjoy!

4
servings

290

25 min

Vegan Mediterranean Orzo Salad

A refreshing Mediterranean orzo salad with orzo pasta, cherry tomatoes, cucumber, and a lemon-herb dressing.

Ingredients:

- 1 1/2 cups orzo pasta, cooked and cooled
- 1 cup cherry tomatoes, halved
- 1/2 cup cucumber, diced
- 1/4 cup red onion, finely chopped
- 1/4 cup Kalamata olives, sliced
- 1/4 cup fresh parsley, chopped
- 2 tbsp fresh dill, chopped
- 2 tbsp lemon juice
- 2 tbsp olive oil
- Salt and pepper to taste

Directions

1. In a bowl, combine cooked and cooled orzo pasta, cherry tomatoes, cucumber, red onion, Kalamata olives, fresh parsley, and fresh dill.
2. In a separate bowl, whisk together lemon juice, olive oil, salt, and pepper.
3. Drizzle dressing over the orzo salad.
4. Toss to mix well.
5. Chill in the refrigerator for at least 30 minutes to let the flavors meld.
6. Serve the vegan Mediterranean orzo salad cold. Enjoy!

Substitutions

- Add diced avocado for creaminess

4 servings **350** **30 min**

Vegan Greek Pasta with Tofu Feta

Easy

A Greek-inspired pasta dish with tofu feta, Kalamata olives, cherry tomatoes, and a zesty lemon dressing.

Ingredients:

- 8 oz penne pasta, cooked
- 1 cup tofu feta cheese (store-bought or homemade)
- 1 cup cherry tomatoes, halved
- 1/4 cup Kalamata olives, sliced
- 1/4 cup red onion, thinly sliced
- 2 tbsp fresh parsley, chopped
- 2 tbsp lemon juice
- 2 tbsp olive oil
- Salt and pepper to taste

Directions

1. Cook penne pasta according to package instructions until al dente. Drain and set aside.
2. In a large bowl, combine cooked penne pasta, tofu feta cheese, cherry tomatoes, Kalamata olives, red onion, and fresh parsley.
3. In a separate bowl, whisk together lemon juice, olive oil, salt, and pepper.
4. Drizzle dressing over the pasta salad.
5. Toss to mix well.
6. Serve the vegan Greek pasta with tofu feta cold. Enjoy!

Substitutions

- Use store-bought vegan feta

4 servings **340** **20 min**

Easy

Vegan Italian Pesto Pasta

A simple and flavorful Italian pesto pasta with homemade basil pesto, cherry tomatoes, and pine nuts.

Ingredients:

- 8 oz linguine or spaghetti
- 1 cup fresh basil leaves
- 1/4 cup pine nuts
- 2 cloves garlic, minced
- 1/4 cup nutritional yeast
- 1/4 cup olive oil
- 2 tbsp lemon juice
- Salt and pepper to taste
- 1 cup cherry tomatoes, halved
- Vegan Parmesan cheese (optional)

Directions

1. Cook linguine or spaghetti according to package instructions until al dente. Drain and set aside.
2. In a food processor, combine fresh basil leaves, pine nuts, minced garlic, nutritional yeast, olive oil, lemon juice, salt, and pepper.
3. Blend until smooth to make the pesto sauce.
4. Toss cooked pasta with pesto sauce and cherry tomatoes.
5. Serve the vegan Italian pesto pasta hot, garnished with vegan Parmesan cheese if desired. Enjoy!

Substitutions

- Use store-bought vegan pesto

4 servings

360 kcal

40 min

Normal

Vegan Turkish Eggplant and Tomato Pasta

Ingredients:

- 8 oz penne pasta, cooked
- 1 large eggplant, cubed
- 1 can (14 oz) diced tomatoes
- 1/2 cup red bell pepper, diced
- 1/2 cup onion, chopped
- 3 cloves garlic, minced
- 2 tbsp olive oil
- 1 tsp smoked paprika
- 1/2 tsp red pepper flakes (adjust to taste)
- Salt and pepper to taste
- Fresh parsley for garnish

Substitutions

- Add a pinch of sumac for extra flavor

A Turkish-inspired pasta dish with roasted eggplant, tomatoes, and a smoky pepper-infused tomato sauce.

Directions

1. Preheat the oven to 400°F (200°C).
2. In a bowl, toss cubed eggplant with olive oil, smoked paprika, red pepper flakes, salt, and pepper.
3. Spread the eggplant on a baking sheet and roast for 20-25 minutes, or until tender and slightly caramelized.
4. In a large skillet, heat olive oil over medium heat.
5. Add chopped onion and diced red bell pepper. Sauté until softened.
6. Stir in minced garlic and canned diced tomatoes.
7. Simmer for 10 minutes, stirring occasionally.
8. Toss cooked penne pasta with the tomato and pepper sauce.
9. Serve the vegan Turkish eggplant and tomato pasta hot, garnished with fresh parsley. Enjoy!

Chapter 9
Mediterranean Rice Dishes

4 servings

350 kcal

45 min

Vegan Lebanese Mujadara

Normal

Ingredients:

- 1 cup brown or green lentils, rinsed and drained
- 1 cup basmati rice
- 3 cups vegetable broth
- 2 large onions, thinly sliced
- 1/4 cup olive oil
- 1 tsp ground cumin
- 1 tsp ground coriander
- 1/2 tsp ground cinnamon
- Salt and pepper to taste
- Tahini sauce for serving (store-bought or homemade)

Substitutions

- Top with chopped fresh parsley for extra freshness

A comforting Lebanese mujadara with lentils, rice, and caramelized onions, served with a zesty tahini sauce.

Directions

1. In a large pot, heat olive oil over medium heat.
2. Add thinly sliced onions and sauté until golden brown and caramelized (about 20-25 minutes). Remove half of the caramelized onions and set them aside for garnish.
3. Stir in ground cumin, ground coriander, ground cinnamon, salt, and pepper.
4. Add rinsed lentils and vegetable broth. Bring to a boil.
5. Reduce heat, cover, and simmer for 20-25 minutes, or until lentils are tender.
6. Stir in basmati rice.
7. Cover and cook for an additional 15-20 minutes, or until rice is cooked and the liquid is absorbed.
8. Serve the mujadara hot, garnished with reserved caramelized onions and drizzled with tahini sauce. Enjoy!

4 servings   **320**   **25 min**

Easy

Vegan Greek Rice Pilaf

A fragrant Greek rice pilaf with aromatic herbs, onions, and a hint of lemon, served with roasted vegetables.

Ingredients:

- 1 1/2 cups long-grain white rice
- 3 cups vegetable broth
- 1/2 cup red bell pepper, diced
- 1/2 cup zucchini, diced
- 1/2 cup cherry tomatoes, halved
- 1/4 cup red onion, finely chopped
- 2 cloves garlic, minced
- 2 tbsp fresh parsley, chopped
- 2 tbsp fresh dill, chopped
- 2 tbsp olive oil
- 1 tsp lemon zest
- 1 tbsp lemon juice
- Salt and pepper to taste

Directions

1. In a large skillet, heat olive oil over medium heat.
2. Add chopped red bell pepper, zucchini, cherry tomatoes, red onion, and minced garlic. Sauté until vegetables are tender.
3. Stir in long-grain white rice and sauté for 2-3 minutes.
4. Pour in vegetable broth, lemon zest, and lemon juice.
5. Cover and simmer for 15-20 minutes, or until rice is cooked and the liquid is absorbed.
6. Stir in fresh parsley and fresh dill.
7. Season with salt and pepper.
8. Serve the Greek rice pilaf hot, garnished with additional fresh herbs if desired. Enjoy!

Substitutions

- Use brown rice for a nuttier flavor

4 servings

310

45 min

Vegan Moroccan Vegetable Tagine

Normal

A Moroccan-inspired vegetable tagine with a medley of colorful veggies, chickpeas, and aromatic spices.

Ingredients:

- 2 cups butternut squash, diced
- 1 cup eggplant, diced
- 1 cup zucchini, diced
- 1/2 cup red bell pepper, diced
- 1/2 cup yellow bell pepper, diced
- 1/2 cup onion, chopped
- 1/2 cup canned chickpeas, rinsed and drained
- 3 cloves garlic, minced
- 1 can (14 oz) diced tomatoes
- 1/4 cup dried apricots, chopped
- 1/4 cup raisins
- 2 tbsp olive oil
- 1 tsp ground cumin
- 1 tsp ground coriander
- 1/2 tsp ground cinnamon
- 1/2 tsp ground ginger
- 1/4 tsp cayenne pepper (adjust to taste)
- Salt and pepper to taste

Substitutions

- Use sweet potatoes for extra sweetness

Directions

1. In a large skillet or tagine, heat olive oil over medium heat.
2. Add chopped butternut squash, diced eggplant, diced zucchini, diced red bell pepper, diced yellow bell pepper, and chopped onion. Sauté until vegetables are slightly softened.
3. Stir in minced garlic, ground cumin, ground coriander, ground cinnamon, ground ginger, and cayenne pepper.
4. Add canned diced tomatoes, dried apricots, raisins, and canned chickpeas.
5. Cover and simmer for 20-25 minutes, or until vegetables are tender.
6. Season with salt and pepper.
7. Serve the Moroccan vegetable tagine hot. Enjoy!

4
servings

360

35 min

Vegan Italian Risotto with Mushrooms

Ingredients:

- 1 1/2 cups Arborio rice
- 1/2 cup white wine
- 4 cups vegetable broth
- 2 cups mushrooms, sliced
- 1/2 cup onion, chopped
- 2 cloves garlic, minced
- 2 tbsp olive oil
- 2 tbsp nutritional yeast
- 2 tbsp fresh parsley, chopped
- Salt and pepper to taste

Substitutions

- Use vegetable stock instead of white wine

Normal

A creamy Italian risotto with Arborio rice, mushrooms, white wine, and a savory vegetable broth.

Directions

1. In a large skillet, heat olive oil over medium heat.
2. Add chopped onion and minced garlic. Sauté until softened.
3. Stir in sliced mushrooms and cook until they release their moisture and become tender.
4. Add Arborio rice and sauté for 2-3 minutes.
5. Pour in white wine and stir until absorbed.
6. Begin adding vegetable broth, one ladle at a time, stirring continuously and allowing the liquid to be absorbed before adding more. Continue until the rice is creamy and tender (about 20-25 minutes).
7. Stir in nutritional yeast and fresh parsley.
8. Season with salt and pepper.
9. Serve the Italian mushroom risotto hot. Enjoy!

4 servings

340 kcal

30 min

Easy

Vegan Spanish Yellow Rice

A vibrant Spanish yellow rice dish with saffron-infused rice, peas, and bell peppers.

Ingredients:

- 1 1/2 cups long-grain white rice
- 3 cups vegetable broth
- 1/2 cup green peas
- 1/2 cup red bell pepper, diced
- 1/2 cup yellow bell pepper, diced
- 1/2 cup onion, chopped
- 3 cloves garlic, minced
- 2 tbsp olive oil
- 1/4 tsp saffron threads (soaked in 2 tbsp warm water)
- Salt and pepper to taste

Substitutions

- Add vegan chorizo for a spicy twist

Directions

1. In a large skillet, heat olive oil over medium heat.
2. Add chopped onion and minced garlic. Sauté until softened.
3. Stir in diced red bell pepper and diced yellow bell pepper. Cook until slightly tender.
4. Add long-grain white rice and sauté for 2-3 minutes.
5. Pour in vegetable broth and soaked saffron threads with their water.
6. Cover and simmer for 15-20 minutes, or until rice is cooked and the liquid is absorbed.
7. Stir in green peas.
8. Season with salt and pepper.
9. Serve the Spanish yellow rice hot. Enjoy!

4 servings

310 kcal

20 min

Vegan Mediterranean Rice Salad

Easy

A refreshing Mediterranean rice salad with fluffy rice, cucumber, cherry tomatoes, and a lemony dressing.

Ingredients:

- 1 1/2 cups cooked long-grain white rice, cooled
- 1 cup cucumber, diced
- 1 cup cherry tomatoes, halved
- 1/4 cup red onion, finely chopped
- 1/4 cup Kalamata olives, sliced
- 2 tbsp fresh parsley, chopped
- 2 tbsp fresh mint, chopped
- 2 tbsp lemon juice
- 2 tbsp olive oil
- Salt and pepper to taste

Directions

1. In a bowl, combine cooked and cooled long-grain white rice, diced cucumber, cherry tomatoes, red onion, Kalamata olives, fresh parsley, and fresh mint.
2. In a separate bowl, whisk together lemon juice, olive oil, salt, and pepper.
3. Drizzle dressing over the rice salad.
4. Toss to mix well.
5. Chill in the refrigerator for at least 30 minutes to let the flavors meld.
6. Serve the Mediterranean rice salad cold. Enjoy!

Substitutions

- Add chickpeas for extra protein and texture

4
servings

330

35 min

Easy

Vegan Turkish Pilaf with Chickpeas

A Turkish-style pilaf with fragrant rice, chickpeas, and a blend of spices, served with a creamy tahini sauce.

Ingredients:

- 1 1/2 cups long-grain white rice
- 3 cups vegetable broth
- 1 can (14 oz) chickpeas, rinsed and drained
- 1/2 cup red bell pepper, diced
- 1/2 cup onion, chopped
- 3 cloves garlic, minced
- 2 tbsp olive oil
- 1 tsp ground cumin
- 1/2 tsp ground coriander
- 1/2 tsp paprika
- Salt and pepper to taste
- Tahini sauce for serving (store-bought or homemade)

Substitutions

- Top with toasted pine nuts for extra crunch

Directions

1. In a large skillet, heat olive oil over medium heat.
2. Add chopped onion and minced garlic. Sauté until softened.
3. Stir in diced red bell pepper and cook until slightly tender.
4. Add long-grain white rice and sauté for 2-3 minutes.
5. Pour in vegetable broth.
6. Add chickpeas, ground cumin, ground coriander, paprika, salt, and pepper.
7. Cover and simmer for 15-20 minutes, or until rice is cooked and the liquid is absorbed.
8. Serve the Turkish pilaf with chickpeas hot, drizzled with tahini sauce. Enjoy!

4 servings

350 kcal

40 min

Vegan Italian Risotto with Asparagus

mmmmmmmm

Creamy Italian risotto with Arborio rice, tender asparagus, white wine, and a hint of lemon zest.

Ingredients:

- 1 1/2 cups Arborio rice
- 1/2 cup white wine
- 4 cups vegetable broth
- 1 bunch asparagus, trimmed and cut into bite-sized pieces
- 1/2 cup onion, chopped
- 2 cloves garlic, minced
- 2 tbsp olive oil
- 2 tbsp nutritional yeast
- 2 tbsp fresh parsley, chopped
- 1 tsp lemon zest
- Salt and pepper to taste

Directions

1. In a large skillet, heat olive oil over medium heat.
2. Add chopped onion and minced garlic. Sauté until softened.
3. Stir in Arborio rice and sauté for 2-3 minutes.
4. Pour in white wine and stir until absorbed.
5. Begin adding vegetable broth, one ladle at a time, stirring continuously and allowing the liquid to be absorbed before adding more. Continue until the rice is creamy and tender (about 20-25 minutes).
6. In the last 5 minutes of cooking, add bite-sized pieces of asparagus and stir until they are tender-crisp.
7. Stir in nutritional yeast, lemon zest, fresh parsley, salt, and pepper.
8. Serve the Italian asparagus risotto hot. Enjoy!

Substitutions

- Use green beans or peas as a substitute for asparagus

4 servings   **320**   **30 min**

Easy

Vegan Greek Spanakorizo

A Greek spinach and rice dish (Spanakorizo) cooked with aromatic herbs, lemon juice, and olive oil.

Ingredients:

- 1 1/2 cups long-grain white rice
- 3 cups vegetable broth
- 1 bunch spinach, chopped
- 1/2 cup onion, chopped
- 2 cloves garlic, minced
- 2 tbsp olive oil
- 2 tbsp fresh dill, chopped
- 2 tbsp fresh mint, chopped
- 2 tbsp lemon juice
- Salt and pepper to taste

Substitutions

- Use brown rice for a nuttier flavor

Directions

1. In a large skillet, heat olive oil over medium heat.
2. Add chopped onion and minced garlic. Sauté until softened.
3. Stir in chopped spinach and cook until wilted.
4. Add long-grain white rice and sauté for 2-3 minutes.
5. Pour in vegetable broth and lemon juice.
6. Cover and simmer for 15-20 minutes, or until rice is cooked and the liquid is absorbed.
7. Stir in fresh dill and fresh mint.
8. Season with salt and pepper.
9. Serve the Greek Spanakorizo hot. Enjoy!

4 servings

360

35 min

Vegan Moroccan Saffron Rice with Almonds

Fragrant Moroccan saffron rice with toasted almonds, dried fruits, and a blend of exotic spices.

Ingredients:

- 1 1/2 cups long-grain white rice
- 3 cups vegetable broth
- 1/4 cup slivered almonds, toasted
- 1/4 cup dried apricots, chopped
- 1/4 cup raisins
- 1/4 cup red onion, finely chopped
- 2 cloves garlic, minced
- 2 tbsp olive oil
- 1/4 tsp saffron threads (soaked in 2 tbsp warm water)
- 1/2 tsp ground cinnamon
- 1/2 tsp ground cumin
- Salt and pepper to taste

Directions

1. In a large skillet, heat olive oil over medium heat.
2. Add chopped red onion and minced garlic. Sauté until softened.
3. Stir in long-grain white rice and sauté for 2-3 minutes.
4. Pour in vegetable broth, soaked saffron threads with their water, ground cinnamon, ground cumin, salt, and pepper.
5. Cover and simmer for 15-20 minutes, or until rice is cooked and the liquid is absorbed.
6. Stir in toasted slivered almonds, chopped dried apricots, and raisins.
7. Serve the Moroccan saffron rice hot. Enjoy!

Substitutions

- Use pine nuts instead of almonds

Chapter 10
Mediterranean Grilled and Roasted

4
servings

280

45 min

Easy

Vegan Greek Lemon Potatoes

~~~~~~~~~~~~~~~

Ingredients:

- 4 large russet potatoes, peeled and cut into wedges
- 1/4 cup olive oil
- 2 lemons, juiced
- 4 cloves garlic, minced
- 2 tsp dried oregano
- 1 tsp dried thyme
- Salt and pepper to taste

Tender potatoes roasted with olive oil, lemon juice, and aromatic herbs, capturing the essence of Greek cuisine.

Directions

1. Preheat the oven to 400°F (200°C).
2. In a large bowl, combine potato wedges, olive oil, lemon juice, minced garlic, dried oregano, dried thyme, salt, and pepper. Toss to coat evenly.
3. Transfer the seasoned potatoes to a baking sheet, arranging them in a single layer.
4. Roast for 35-40 minutes, flipping the potatoes halfway through, or until they are golden and tender.
5. Serve the Greek lemon potatoes hot. Enjoy!

Substitutions

- Add fresh rosemary for extra flavor

4 servings

230

30 min

Vegan Moroccan Vegetable Kebabs

Ingredients:

- 2 zucchinis, cut into rounds
- 1 red bell pepper, cut into chunks
- 1 yellow bell pepper, cut into chunks
- 1 red onion, cut into chunks
- 1 cup cherry tomatoes
- 1/4 cup olive oil
- 2 cloves garlic, minced
- 1 tsp ground cumin
- 1 tsp ground coriander
- 1/2 tsp smoked paprika
- 1/2 tsp ground cinnamon
- Salt and pepper to taste
- Wooden skewers, soaked in water

Substitutions

- Add tofu or tempeh for additional protein

Flavorful vegetable kebabs with a Moroccan twist, marinated in spices and grilled to perfection.

Directions

1. In a bowl, prepare the marinade by combining olive oil, minced garlic, ground cumin, ground coriander, smoked paprika, ground cinnamon, salt, and pepper.
2. Thread the marinated vegetables onto soaked wooden skewers, alternating between zucchini rounds, red bell pepper, yellow bell pepper, red onion chunks, and cherry tomatoes.
3. Preheat a grill or grill pan over medium-high heat.
4. Grill vegetable kebabs for 3-4 minutes per side, or until they have grill marks and are tender.
5. Serve the Moroccan vegetable kebabs hot. Enjoy!

4 servings

340 kcal

45 min

Vegan Italian Stuffed Bell Peppers

Ingredients:

- 4 large bell peppers, any color
- 1 cup Arborio rice
- 2 cups vegetable broth
- 1/2 cup onion, chopped
- 1/2 cup zucchini, diced
- 1/2 cup cherry tomatoes, halved
- 1/4 cup Kalamata olives, sliced
- 2 cloves garlic, minced
- 2 tbsp olive oil
- 2 tsp Italian seasoning
- Salt and pepper to taste

Substitutions

- Top with vegan cheese for extra indulgence

Normal

Bell peppers stuffed with a savory mixture of rice, vegetables, and Italian spices, baked to perfection.

Directions

1. Preheat the oven to 375°F (190°C).
2. Cut the tops off the bell peppers and remove the seeds and membranes. Set aside.
3. In a large skillet, heat olive oil over medium heat.
4. Add chopped onion and minced garlic. Sauté until softened.
5. Stir in Arborio rice and sauté for 2-3 minutes.
6. Pour in vegetable broth and add diced zucchini, halved cherry tomatoes, sliced Kalamata olives, Italian seasoning, salt, and pepper.
7. Cover and simmer for 15-20 minutes, or until rice is cooked and the liquid is absorbed.
8. Stuff the bell peppers with the cooked rice mixture.
9. Place stuffed peppers in a baking dish and cover with aluminum foil.
10. Bake for 20-25 minutes.
11. Serve the vegan Italian stuffed bell peppers hot. Enjoy!

4 servings   **240**   **25 min**

Easy

Vegan Lebanese Grilled Eggplant

Ingredients:

- 2 large eggplants, sliced into rounds
- 1/4 cup olive oil
- 2 cloves garlic, minced
- 2 tbsp lemon juice
- 2 tbsp fresh parsley, chopped
- 2 tbsp fresh mint, chopped
- Salt and pepper to taste

Grilled eggplant slices with a Lebanese twist, marinated in garlic, lemon juice, and fresh herbs.

Directions

1. In a bowl, prepare the marinade by combining olive oil, minced garlic, lemon juice, fresh parsley, fresh mint, salt, and pepper.
2. Brush both sides of eggplant slices generously with the marinade.
3. Preheat a grill or grill pan over medium-high heat.
4. Grill eggplant slices for 2-3 minutes per side, or until they have grill marks and are tender.
5. Serve the Lebanese grilled eggplant hot. Enjoy!

Substitutions

- Add a pinch of sumac for an extra Lebanese touch

4
servings

170

30 min

Vegan Spanish Grilled Portobello Mushrooms

Easy

Juicy Portobello mushrooms marinated in Spanish flavors, grilled to smoky perfection.

Ingredients:

- 4 large Portobello mushrooms, stems removed
- 1/4 cup olive oil
- 2 cloves garlic, minced
- 2 tbsp balsamic vinegar
- 1 tsp smoked paprika
- 1/2 tsp ground cumin
- Salt and pepper to taste

Directions

1. In a bowl, prepare the marinade by combining olive oil, minced garlic, balsamic vinegar, smoked paprika, ground cumin, salt, and pepper.
2. Brush both sides of Portobello mushrooms generously with the marinade.
3. Preheat a grill or grill pan over medium-high heat.
4. Grill Portobello mushrooms for 3-4 minutes per side, or until they have grill marks and are tender.
5. Serve the Spanish grilled Portobello mushrooms hot. Enjoy!

Substitutions

- Drizzle with vegan chimichurri sauce for extra flavor

4 servings

120 kcal

25 min

Vegan Mediterranean Roasted Red Pepper Dip

Easy

Creamy roasted red pepper dip with a medley of Mediterranean flavors, perfect for dipping or spreading.

Ingredients:

- 2 large red bell peppers, roasted, peeled, and seeded
- 1/2 cup raw cashews, soaked
- 2 cloves garlic, minced
- 2 tbsp olive oil
- 2 tbsp lemon juice
- 1 tsp smoked paprika
- 1/2 tsp ground cumin
- Salt and pepper to taste
- Fresh parsley for garnish (optional)

Directions

1. In a food processor, combine roasted red bell peppers, soaked raw cashews, minced garlic, olive oil, lemon juice, smoked paprika, ground cumin, salt, and pepper.
2. Blend until smooth and creamy.
3. Transfer the roasted red pepper dip to a serving bowl.
4. Garnish with fresh parsley if desired.
5. Serve the Mediterranean roasted red pepper dip with pita bread, crackers, or fresh vegetables. Enjoy!

Substitutions

- Use almonds or sunflower seeds if allergic to cashews

4 servings   **280**   **40 min**

Vegan Greek Grilled Tofu

Ingredients:

- 1 block (14 oz) extra-firm tofu, pressed and sliced
- 1/4 cup olive oil
- 2 lemons, juiced
- 4 cloves garlic, minced
- 2 tsp dried oregano
- Salt and pepper to taste
- Tzatziki sauce for serving (store-bought or homemade)

Substitutions

- Use tempeh or seitan for a different protein source

Easy

Grilled tofu marinated in Greek flavors with lemon, garlic, and oregano, served with a tangy tzatziki sauce.

Directions

1. In a bowl, prepare the marinade by combining olive oil, lemon juice, minced garlic, dried oregano, salt, and pepper.
2. Place sliced tofu in a shallow dish and pour the marinade over it. Let it marinate for at least 30 minutes, turning the tofu slices occasionally.
3. Preheat a grill or grill pan over medium-high heat.
4. Grill tofu slices for 2-3 minutes per side, or until they have grill marks and are heated through.
5. Serve the Greek grilled tofu hot, drizzled with tzatziki sauce. Enjoy!

4 servings

180 kcal

30 min

Easy

Vegan Italian Roasted Vegetable Medley

Ingredients:

- 2 cups cherry tomatoes
- 1 cup zucchini, sliced
- 1 cup bell peppers (mix of red and yellow), sliced
- 1 cup red onion, sliced
- 1/4 cup olive oil
- 2 cloves garlic, minced
- 1 tsp dried basil
- 1 tsp dried oregano
- 2 tbsp balsamic vinegar
- Salt and pepper to taste

A colorful medley of roasted Italian vegetables, seasoned with herbs and balsamic vinegar.

Directions

1. Preheat the oven to 425°F (220°C).
2. In a large bowl, combine cherry tomatoes, sliced zucchini, sliced bell peppers, sliced red onion, minced garlic, dried basil, dried oregano, olive oil, balsamic vinegar, salt, and pepper. Toss to coat evenly.
3. Spread the seasoned vegetables on a baking sheet in a single layer.
4. Roast for 20-25 minutes, or until the vegetables are tender and slightly caramelized.
5. Serve the Italian roasted vegetable medley hot. Enjoy!

Substitutions

- Add roasted eggplant or asparagus for variety

4 servings

250 kcal

50 min

Vegan Turkish Stuffed Grape Leaves

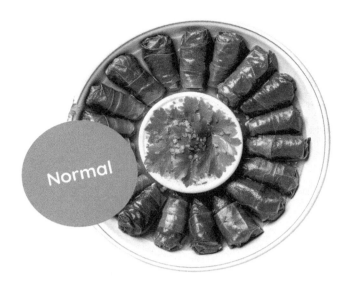

Normal

Tender grape leaves stuffed with a flavorful mixture of rice, herbs, and spices, a classic Turkish delicacy.

Ingredients:

- 1 jar (16 oz) grape leaves in brine, drained and rinsed
- 1 cup Arborio rice
- 2 cups vegetable broth
- 1/2 cup onion, finely chopped
- 1/4 cup fresh dill, chopped
- 1/4 cup fresh mint, chopped
- 2 cloves garlic, minced
- 2 tbsp olive oil
- 2 tbsp lemon juice
- Salt and pepper to taste

Directions

1. In a large skillet, heat olive oil over medium heat.
2. Add chopped onion and minced garlic. Sauté until softened.
3. Stir in Arborio rice and sauté for 2-3 minutes.
4. Pour in vegetable broth, fresh dill, fresh mint, lemon juice, salt, and pepper.
5. Cover and simmer for 15-20 minutes, or until rice is cooked and the liquid is absorbed.
6. Carefully separate and flatten grape leaves.
7. Place a small spoonful of the rice mixture in the center of each grape leaf and fold the sides in, rolling tightly.
8. Arrange stuffed grape leaves in a deep pot or pan, seam-side down.
9. Add a small amount of vegetable broth to the pot.
10. Cover and simmer on low heat for 15-20 minutes, or until the stuffed grape leaves are tender.
11. Serve the Turkish stuffed grape leaves hot or at room temperature. Enjoy!

Substitutions

- Top with vegan yogurt or tahini sauce for extra richness

4
servings

190

35 min

Easy

Vegan Moroccan Spiced Cauliflower

〜〜〜〜〜〜〜〜

Ingredients:

- 1 large cauliflower, cut into florets
- 1/4 cup olive oil
- 2 tsp ground cumin
- 1 tsp ground coriander
- 1/2 tsp ground cinnamon
- 1/2 tsp smoked paprika
- 1/4 tsp cayenne pepper (adjust to taste)
- Salt and pepper to taste
- Fresh cilantro for garnish (optional)

Roasted cauliflower florets seasoned with Moroccan spices, creating a flavorful and aromatic side dish.

Directions

1. Preheat the oven to 425°F (220°C).
2. In a large bowl, combine cauliflower florets, olive oil, ground cumin, ground coriander, ground cinnamon, smoked paprika, cayenne pepper, salt, and pepper. Toss to coat evenly.
3. Spread the seasoned cauliflower on a baking sheet in a single layer.
4. Roast for 20-25 minutes, or until the cauliflower is tender and slightly crispy.
5. Garnish with fresh cilantro if desired.
6. Serve the Moroccan spiced cauliflower hot. Enjoy!

Substitutions

- Add chickpeas for added protein and texture

Chapter 11
Mediterranean Sides

8 servings

60

15 min

Vegan Greek Tzatziki

Easy

A creamy and tangy Greek tzatziki sauce made with dairy-free yogurt, cucumber, garlic, and fresh herbs.

Ingredients:

- 2 cups dairy-free yogurt (e.g., almond, soy, or coconut)
- 1 cucumber, grated and squeezed to remove excess liquid
- 3 cloves garlic, minced
- 2 tbsp fresh dill, chopped
- 2 tbsp fresh mint, chopped
- 2 tbsp lemon juice
- 2 tbsp olive oil
- Salt and pepper to taste

Directions

1. In a bowl, combine dairy-free yogurt, grated and squeezed cucumber, minced garlic, fresh dill, fresh mint, lemon juice, olive oil, salt, and pepper.
2. Mix well until all ingredients are thoroughly combined.
3. Refrigerate the vegan Greek tzatziki for at least 30 minutes to let the flavors meld.
4. Serve the tzatziki sauce chilled, as a dip, or with your favorite Mediterranean dishes. Enjoy!

Substitutions

- Use vegan sour cream as an alternative

8
servings

90

10 min

Vegan Moroccan Spiced Olives

Ingredients:

- 2 cups mixed olives (green and black)
- 2 tbsp olive oil
- 1 tsp ground cumin
- 1/2 tsp ground coriander
- 1/2 tsp smoked paprika
- 1/4 tsp cayenne pepper (adjust to taste)
- Zest of 1 lemon
- Fresh cilantro for garnish (optional)
- Lemon wedges for serving (optional)

Easy

A medley of olives marinated in Moroccan spices, creating a flavorful and aromatic side dish.

Directions

1. In a bowl, combine mixed olives, olive oil, ground cumin, ground coriander, smoked paprika, cayenne pepper, and lemon zest. Toss to coat the olives evenly with the spices and oil.
2. Garnish with fresh cilantro if desired.
3. Serve the vegan Moroccan spiced olives as a side dish with lemon wedges for extra zing. Enjoy!

Substitutions

- Add crushed red pepper flakes for extra heat

6
servings

120

15 min

Vegan Italian Bruschetta

Ingredients:

- 1 baguette, sliced into rounds
- 4 large tomatoes, diced
- 4 cloves garlic, minced
- 1/4 cup fresh basil, chopped
- 2 tbsp balsamic glaze
- 2 tbsp olive oil
- Salt and pepper to taste

Classic Italian bruschetta with diced tomatoes, fresh basil, garlic, and balsamic glaze on toasted baguette slices.

Directions

1. Preheat the oven to 375°F (190°C).
2. Arrange baguette slices on a baking sheet and drizzle with olive oil.
3. Toast in the oven for 5-7 minutes or until the bread is crisp and slightly golden.
4. In a bowl, combine diced tomatoes, minced garlic, fresh basil, balsamic glaze, olive oil, salt, and pepper. Mix well.
5. Spoon the tomato mixture onto the toasted baguette slices.
6. Serve the vegan Italian bruschetta as an appetizer or side dish. Enjoy!

Substitutions

- Add diced red onion for extra flavor

8
servings

70

10 min

Vegan Lebanese Hummus

Ingredients:

- 2 cans (15 oz each) chickpeas, drained and rinsed
- 1/2 cup tahini
- 3 cloves garlic, minced
- 3 tbsp lemon juice
- 2 tbsp olive oil
- 1/2 tsp ground cumin
- Salt and pepper to taste
- Fresh parsley for garnish (optional)
- Paprika for garnish (optional)
- Olive oil for drizzling (optional)

Substitutions

- Adjust lemon juice and garlic to taste

Easy

Creamy Lebanese hummus made with chickpeas, tahini, lemon juice, and garlic, perfect for dipping or spreading.

Directions

1. In a food processor, combine chickpeas, tahini, minced garlic, lemon juice, olive oil, ground cumin, salt, and pepper.
2. Blend until the hummus is smooth and creamy, adding a splash of water if needed to reach the desired consistency.
3. Transfer the Lebanese hummus to a serving bowl.
4. Garnish with fresh parsley, paprika, and a drizzle of olive oil if desired.
5. Serve the hummus with pita bread, crackers, or fresh vegetables. Enjoy!

6 servings

220 kcal

40 min

Vegan Spanish Patatas Bravas

Crispy potato cubes served with a smoky and spicy tomato sauce, a classic Spanish tapas dish.

Ingredients:

- 4 large potatoes, peeled and cut into small cubes
- 2 tbsp olive oil
- 1 tsp smoked paprika
- Salt and pepper to taste
- For the tomato sauce:
  - 1 can (14 oz) diced tomatoes
  - 2 cloves garlic, minced
  - 1/2 tsp smoked paprika
  - 1/4 tsp cayenne pepper (adjust to taste)
  - 1/4 cup vegan mayonnaise (optional)
  - Olive oil for drizzling (optional)

Substitutions

- Top with chopped fresh parsley for freshness

Directions

For the crispy potatoes:
1. Preheat the oven to 425°F (220°C).
2. In a large bowl, combine potato cubes, olive oil, smoked paprika, salt, and pepper. Toss to coat the potatoes evenly.
3. Spread the potatoes on a baking sheet in a single layer.
4. Roast for 30-35 minutes, or until the potatoes are crispy and golden, flipping them halfway through.
For the tomato sauce:
5. In a saucepan, combine diced tomatoes, minced garlic, smoked paprika, and cayenne pepper. Cook over medium heat for about 10 minutes, stirring occasionally, until the sauce thickens.
6. Serve the crispy potatoes with the tomato sauce drizzled on top. Optionally, drizzle with vegan mayonnaise and a little olive oil. Enjoy!

8 servings

180 kcal

40 min

Vegan Mediterranean Dolmas

Ingredients:

- 1 jar (16 oz) grape leaves in brine, drained and rinsed
- 1 cup Arborio rice
- 2 cups vegetable broth
- 1/2 cup onion, finely chopped
- 1/4 cup fresh dill, chopped
- 1/4 cup fresh mint, chopped
- 2 cloves garlic, minced
- 2 tbsp olive oil
- 2 tbsp lemon juice
- Salt and pepper to taste

Substitutions

- Top with vegan yogurt or tahini sauce for extra richness

Grape leaves stuffed with a flavorful mixture of rice, herbs, and spices, a classic Mediterranean delicacy.

Directions

1. In a large skillet, heat olive oil over medium heat.
2. Add chopped onion and minced garlic. Sauté until softened.
3. Stir in Arborio rice and sauté for 2-3 minutes.
4. Pour in vegetable broth, fresh dill, fresh mint, lemon juice, salt, and pepper.
5. Cover and simmer for 15-20 minutes, or until rice is cooked and the liquid is absorbed.
6. Carefully separate and flatten grape leaves.
7. Place a small spoonful of the rice mixture in the center of each grape leaf and fold the sides in, rolling tightly.
8. Arrange stuffed grape leaves in a deep pot or pan, seam-side down.
9. Add a small amount of vegetable broth to the pot.
10. Cover and simmer on low heat for 15-20 minutes, or until the stuffed grape leaves are tender.
11. Serve the Mediterranean dolmas hot or at room temperature. Enjoy!

8
servings

190

40 min

Vegan Greek Stuffed Grape Leaves

Normal

Ingredients:

- 1 jar (16 oz) grape leaves in brine, drained and rinsed
- 1 cup Arborio rice
- 2 cups vegetable broth
- 1/2 cup onion, finely chopped
- 1/4 cup fresh dill, chopped
- 1/4 cup fresh mint, chopped
- 2 cloves garlic, minced
- 2 tbsp olive oil
- 2 tbsp lemon juice
- Salt and pepper to taste

Substitutions

- Top with vegan yogurt or tahini sauce for extra richness

Tender grape leaves stuffed with a savory mixture of rice and herbs, a classic Greek meze dish.

Directions

1. In a large skillet, heat olive oil over medium heat.
2. Add chopped onion and minced garlic. Sauté until softened.
3. Stir in Arborio rice and sauté for 2-3 minutes.
4. Pour in vegetable broth, fresh dill, fresh mint, lemon juice, salt, and pepper.
5. Cover and simmer for 15-20 minutes, or until rice is cooked and the liquid is absorbed.
6. Carefully separate and flatten grape leaves.
7. Place a small spoonful of the rice mixture in the center of each grape leaf and fold the sides in, rolling tightly.
8. Arrange stuffed grape leaves in a deep pot or pan, seam-side down.
9. Add a small amount of vegetable broth to the pot.
10. Cover and simmer on low heat for 15-20 minutes, or until the stuffed grape leaves are tender.
11. Serve the vegan Greek stuffed grape leaves hot or at room temperature. Enjoy!

6
servings

260

15 min

Easy

Vegan Italian Garlic Bread

Ingredients:

- 1 large baguette or Italian bread
- 1/2 cup vegan butter, softened
- 4 cloves garlic, minced
- 2 tbsp fresh parsley, chopped (optional)
- Salt to taste

Crispy and garlicky Italian bread, perfect as a side or for dipping in marinara sauce.

Directions

1. Preheat the oven to 375°F (190°C).
2. Slice the baguette or Italian bread in half lengthwise.
3. In a bowl, mix softened vegan butter, minced garlic, chopped fresh parsley (if using), and a pinch of salt.
4. Spread the garlic butter mixture evenly over the cut sides of the bread.
5. Place the bread halves on a baking sheet, cut side up.
6. Bake in the oven for 10-12 minutes or until the bread is toasted and the garlic butter is melted and bubbly.
7. Slice and serve the vegan Italian garlic bread hot. Enjoy!

Substitutions

- Use olive oil instead of vegan butter

6 servings **110** **40 min**

Easy

Vegan Turkish Baba Ghanoush

Smoky and creamy roasted eggplant dip with tahini, garlic, and lemon, a Turkish favorite.

Ingredients:

- 2 large eggplants
- 1/4 cup tahini
- 3 cloves garlic, minced
- 2 tbsp lemon juice
- 2 tbsp olive oil
- 1/2 tsp ground cumin
- Salt and pepper to taste
- Fresh parsley for garnish (optional)
- Olive oil for drizzling (optional)
- Pomegranate seeds for garnish (optional)

Directions

1. Preheat the oven to 400°F (200°C).
2. Prick the eggplants with a fork and place them on a baking sheet.
3. Roast the eggplants in the oven for 30-35 minutes or until they are soft and the skin is charred.
4. Let the roasted eggplants cool slightly, then peel off the charred skin.
5. In a food processor, combine the roasted eggplant flesh, tahini, minced garlic, lemon juice, olive oil, ground cumin, salt, and pepper.
6. Blend until smooth and creamy.
7. Transfer the Turkish baba ghanoush to a serving bowl.
8. Garnish with fresh parsley, a drizzle of olive oil, and pomegranate seeds if desired.
9. Serve the baba ghanoush with pita bread, crackers, or fresh vegetables. Enjoy!

Substitutions

- Add smoked paprika for extra smokiness

6 servings

250

25 min

Vegan Moroccan Couscous with Dried Fruit

Normal

Fluffy couscous infused with Moroccan spices and studded with dried fruit, a sweet and savory side dish.

Ingredients:

- 2 cups couscous
- 2 1/2 cups vegetable broth
- 1/2 cup dried apricots, chopped
- 1/2 cup raisins
- 1/4 cup slivered almonds, toasted
- 1/4 cup red onion, finely chopped
- 2 cloves garlic, minced
- 2 tbsp olive oil
- 1/4 tsp saffron threads (soaked in 2 tbsp warm water)
- 1/2 tsp ground cinnamon
- 1/2 tsp ground cumin
- Salt and pepper to taste

Substitutions

- Use couscous of your choice

Directions

1. In a large skillet, heat olive oil over medium heat.
2. Add chopped red onion and minced garlic. Sauté until softened.
3. Stir in couscous and sauté for 2-3 minutes.
4. Pour in vegetable broth, soaked saffron threads with their water, ground cinnamon, ground cumin, salt, and pepper.
5. Cover and simmer for 5-7 minutes, or until the couscous is tender and has absorbed the liquid.
6. Fluff the couscous with a fork and stir in dried apricots, raisins, and toasted slivered almonds.
7. Serve the Moroccan couscous with dried fruit hot as a side dish. Enjoy!

We have a small favor to ask

Dear fellow culinary voyagers,

As we close the pages of our "Mediterranean Plant-Based Cookbook: From Olive Grove to Table," I want to express my heartfelt gratitude to each and every one of you who joined us on this epicurean adventure. Together, we've embarked on a flavorful journey through the sun-kissed lands of the Mediterranean, savoring the bounties of plant-based cuisine that this region so generously offers.

Before we part ways, I have a small favor to ask, one that carries immense significance for a small, passionate publishing team like ours. In the realm of cookbooks, reviews are akin to the secret spices that elevate a dish from good to extraordinary. They are the lifeblood of our creative process and the fuel that keeps our culinary fire burning.

If our recipes have allowed you to experience the magic of Mediterranean cuisine in its purest form, if you've tasted the freshness of a Greek salad under the Mediterranean sun, the comfort of a Sicilian caponata, or the fragrant allure of a Moroccan tagine, then we kindly ask for your support.

I invite you to take a moment to revisit the platform or app through which you acquired this cookbook. There, you'll find the review button, eagerly awaiting your feedback. A simple star rating along with a few words sharing your thoughts and experiences can have a profound impact, much like the symphony of flavors in a perfectly crafted Mediterranean dish.

Please understand that as a small, independent publisher, every review is a glimmer of light on a dark, stormy night. Your words can inspire others to embark on their own culinary odyssey through the world of plant-based Mediterranean delights.

I want to emphasize that every review, whether long or short, a shower of stars or just one, is treasured by us. In the intricate dance of flavors that define Mediterranean cuisine, even the most skilled chefs may occasionally step on each other's toes. We've poured our hearts and souls into crafting this cookbook, and while our aim is excellence, we understand that the occasional hiccup is part of our creative journey.

From the depths of my heart, I offer my sincerest thanks for choosing the "Mediterranean Plant-Based Cookbook." Your support not only nourishes our culinary passion but also fuels our desire to continue exploring and creating. We eagerly anticipate the day when our next cookbook graces your kitchen, prepared to whisk you away on another epicurean expedition.

For now, as you relish the vibrant and healthful delights of Mediterranean cuisine, may your review be a guiding star for future culinary adventurers. Thank you for being an essential part of our culinary journey, and here's to the timeless joys of plant-based Mediterranean cuisine.